For you ♡
from me
Jan 27th 2024

# NAPOLEON
# HIS LIFE,
# HIS BATTLES,
# HIS EMPIRE

**DAVID CHANTERANNE & EMMANUELLE PAPOT**

WELBECK

# Contents

This edition published in 2023 by Welbeck, an imprint of Welbeck Non-Fiction Limited, part of Welbeck Publishing Group. Offices in: London - 20 Mortimer Street, London W1T 3JW & Sydney - Level 17, 207 Kent St, Sydney NSW 2000 Australia First published in 2010 by Carlton Books Ltd.

Text & design © Welbeck Non-Fiction Limited 2010, 2018, 2023

A CIP catalogue record for this book is available from the British Library.

UK ISBN: 978-1-80279-842-5
US ISBN: 978-0-23300-573-7

Printed in Dubai

10 9 8 7 6 5 4 3 2 1

# Introduction

François-René de Chateaubriand, in his *Mémoires d'Outre-Tombe*, wrote that "on the 5th [May 1821], at eleven minutes to six in the evening, in the midst of winds, rain and the crashing of the waves, Bonaparte rendered up to God the mightiest breath of life that ever animated human clay".

Although views of Napoleon may diverge, one thing is clear to all: he is one of the most famous historical figures of all time.

It is now impossible to count how many books and studies have been devoted to him all over the world. Not a single aspect of his life or personality has escaped close scrutiny and analysis by people fed by a fascination (legitimate or otherwise) for him.

And his ambition, exceptional destiny and downfall are indeed fascinating.

How could a mediocre student without a cent, with a thick Corsican accent, go on to become the conqueror of Europe, on equal terms with the descendants of Charles V and Peter the Great?

As a believer in his lucky star from a very early age, he declared himself a man of destiny whilst in Egypt and never wavered in this conviction, to the point of obstinacy.

Although his reign as Emperor was short, merely fifteen years, these years proved decisive, as they brought with them far-reaching reforms of France in political and diplomatic spheres, as well as on economic, military and cultural planes.

Beyond the frontiers of Europe and even beyond the oceans, he came to mould the world in his image.

A tutelary figure for some, a man of conviction for others, Napoleon was also an excellent communicator who left to posterity not only numerous writings but also a unique, astutely crafted image that is instantly recognizable. This image was widely popularized by a constant stream of artworks devoted to him, particularly vernacular lithographs but also caricatures.

Napoleon had an unparalleled way with words. When he wrote, in 1791, that "men of genius are meteors destined to burn to light up their century", he would never say anything truer, without realizing that this dictum would be applied to him as an incredible prophecy. After his death, the Romantic writers took possession of his extraordinary career, with Victor Hugo even comparing him to a "modern Prometheus".

This book seeks, in 27 magnificently illustrated chapters containing beautifully reproduced documents, to remind us of what his destiny contributed to history.

David Chanteranne and Emmanuelle Papot

*This book is dedicated to our son Malo.*

## The Campaigns of Napoleon, 1796–1815

| | |
|---|---|
| | French Empire |
| | states ruled by members of Napoleon's family and other other dependent states |

**battles and campaigns of**

| | |
|---|---|
| ⊗ → | The War in Italy, 1796 French campaigns |
| ⊗ → | The War of the Second Coalition French campaigns |
| ⊗ → | The War of the Third Coalition French campaigns |
| ⬤ → | The Austrian War of 1809 French campaigns |
| ⊗ ↓ | The Peninsular War Spanish uprisings |
| ⊗ →→ | The Russian campaign, 1812 French advances French retreats |
| ⊗ → | The War of Liberation from French rule, 1813 Allied campaigns |
| ⊗ → | The defence of France, 1814 Allied campaigns |
| ⬤ → | The War of the 100 Days, 1815 French campaigns |
| ✕ | major naval battles |
| — | frontiers, 1812 |

UNITED

KINGDOM

North Sea

Glasgow
Edinburgh
Newcastle
Dublin
Liverpool
Bristol
London
Plymouth
Portsmouth
Amsterdam
Antwerp
Boulogne
Waterloo · Brussels
Quatre-Bras · Ligny
Laon · Craonne
Château-Thierry · Rheims
Rouen · Vauchamps
Paris · Champaubert · St Dizier
Montmirail · La Roth
Montereau · Arcis-sur-Aub
Bar-sur-Aub
La Fère · Brienne-
Champenoise · le-Château

Camperdown ✕ 1797

Channel Is.

Brest

Nantes
Orléans
Loire

FRENCH

EMPIRE

NEUCHÂTEL
Geneva
Lyons

Atlantic Ocean

✕ Cape Finisterre 1805

Aix Roads 1809 ✕
Rochefort

Corunna 1809 ⊗

Oviedo

Bordeaux

Bilbao
San Sebastián 1813 ⊗
Bayonne 1814 ⊗
1814 ⊗ Toulouse
Pamplona 1813 ⊗
Sahagun 1808 ⊗
Burgos 1812 ⊗
Oporto ⊗ 1809
Douro
Valladolid
Saragossa
1809 ⊗
Almeida 1811 ⊗
Buçaco 1810 ⊗
Salamanca 1812 ⊗
Cuidad Rodrigo 1812
Fuentes de Oñoro 1811
Vimeiro 1808 ⊗
Tagus
Girona 1809 ⊗
Barcelona
Marseilles
Toulon
Turi
Montenc
Mondovi

CATALONIA

Alcalá de Henares
Talavera 1809 ⊗
Madrid (captured 1808)
Badajoz 1811, 1812 ⊗
Tarragona 1811 ⊗
Tortosa
Lisbon (captured 1809)
PORTUGAL
Albuera 1811

SPAIN

1811 ⊗ Valencia

Balearics

Cape St Vincent 1797 ✕

Cordova
Bailén 1808 ⊗
Seville
Granada
Cartagena

KINGDOM
OF
SARDIN

Cadiz 1801 ✕
Cadiz
Barrosa 1808 ⊗
Trafalgar 1805 ✕
Tangier
Gibraltar
Algeciras 1801 ✕

Mediterranean Sea

Cagli

NORWAY

SWEDEN

Gothenburg

Aarhus

Copenhagen × Copenhagen 1801, 1807

DENMARK

Lübeck

Hamburg

Hanover

WESTPHALIA

CONFEDERATION OF THE RHINE

Frankfurt

Auerstädt 1806 × ×
Jena 1806 ×

Ulm 1805 ×

HELVETIC REPUBLIC

Munich

Milan ×
Lonato × Rivoli × Bassano ×
Lodi ×
Castiglione ×
Marengo Arcola ×
1800

Bologna

LUCCA

Florence

Elba

MBINO

ica

Rome

KINGDOM OF ITALY

KINGDOM OF NAPLES

Naples

Taranto

Corfu

FINLAND

Helsinki

St Petersburg

Stockholm

Pskov

Revel

Riga

Baltic Sea

to Sweden

Danzig

Stettin

PRUSSIA

Berlin
Grossbeeren

Battle of the Nations
Leipzig

Bautzen ×
Dresden ×
Lützen ×
Kulm ×
Katzbach ×
Breslau

Prague

BOHEMIA

Nuremberg

Abensburg–Eckmühl 1809
Hohenlinden 1800 ×

AUSTRIAN EMPIRE

Austerlitz 1805 ×

Brünn

Wagram 1809 ×
Aspern-Essling 1809 ×
Vienna

Salzburg

Innsbruck

Graz

Buda Pest

HUNGARY

Trieste

Venice

ILLYRIAN

Zagreb

Sava

TRANSYLVANIA

Belgrade

WALLACHIA

Danube

SAN MARINO

Spalato

PROVINCES

Adriatic Sea

Danube

OTTOMAN EMPIRE

Dvinsk
Dvina

Tilsit
Nieman

Königsberg
Eylau 1807
Friedland 1807 ×
Hoff 1807 × Heilsberg 1807 ×
Ionkovo 1807 ×

Vilna

Posen

Tscharnovo 1807
Warsaw
Pultusk 1807 ×
Praga 1807 ×

GRAND DUCHY OF WARSAW

Vistula

Oder

Cracow

Brest-Litovsk

Minsk

Berezina

Orsha

Krasnoi ×

Smolensk (captured 1812)

Vitebsk

Valutino ×

Vyazma ×

Borodino ×

Moscow (captured 1812)

Tarutino ×
Maloyaroslavets

Dnieper

RUSSIAN EMPIRE

Kursk

Kharkov

Kiev

Dniester

BESSARABIA

MOLDAVIA

Don

Black Sea

# The Birth of Napoleon

**" ... I was born when the fatherland was dying. Thirty thousand Frenchmen spewed up on our shores, drowning the throne of liberty in rivers of blood, this was the hideous sight that first struck my gaze. The cries of the dying, the groans of the oppressed and tears of despair surrounded my cradle from the moment of my birth."**

With these words, written thirty years after Corsica's union with France, Napoleon Bonaparte recorded the fact that his destiny was rooted in his Corsican descent.

Of Italian origin, the Buonapartes had actually been established on the "Island of Beauty" for less than 300 years. Some sources have linked them to a branch from Sarzana, exiled at the time of the Guelfes and the Gibelins, and to another branch that was said to have lived in Florence.

In 1768 Corsica, previously under Genoese rule, had just become French. Every Corsican family had to make a very difficult choice: whether to serve their new masters under the authority of the governor, the Comte de Marbeuf, and take advantage of the many opportunities offered by the new regime, or to join the insurgents led by General Pasquale Paoli and risk living outside the law. Carlo and his wife Letizia (who had married in 1764) at first chose to follow their brothers in arms, especially during the battle of Ponte Novo. But the young Letizia was expecting a second son to follow Joseph, who was then only a year old, so Carlo very quickly decided on the more sensible option.

As is well-known, the birth of this second son took place in the town of Ajaccio on 15 August 1769. That day was also the first anniversary of the treaty establishing the union of Corsica and France.

The family had just returned to their home in the rue Saint-Charles following high mass held to celebrate the Assumption of the Virgin Mary. Letizia gave birth in the drawing room, as she did not have time to reach her bedroom on the upper floor. The novelist Stendhal wrote that the child was placed on "one of those old carpets with classical heroes from mythology or the Iliad". A lovely picture, but the boy's mother denied it, saying, "It's a myth. Did he need that?" and adding rather neatly, "We did not have carpets in our Corsican houses, still less at the height of summer than in winter."

Above: *Napoleon's father, Charles Bonaparte, immediately threw his lot in with Pascal Paoli when the French invaded Corsica in 1768, but the defeat at Ponte Novo on 8 May 1769 forced him to make a choice between his heart and his head. Giving top priority to his children's future, Charles decided he would pay allegiance to the King of France, Louis XV.*

Opposite: *Corsica, the island of Napoleon's birth, in the nineteenth century.*

## Carlo Bonaparte (1746–85)

Napoleon's father, who died of cancer when Napoleon was not yet sixteen, had long been a supporter of the idea of Corsican independence, but he did not leave a deep impression on his son. What he did manage to pass on to the boy was his interest in law (he studied in Italy and embarked on a career as a lawyer), a passion for reading and respect for other men. He also did everything possible to give his children a quality education (Napoleon attended the Collège d'Autun followed by the École Militaire de Brienne), thus enabling them to rise above their social status of minor Corsican nobility.

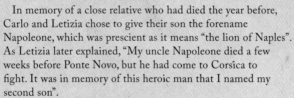

In memory of a close relative who had died the year before, Carlo and Letizia chose to give their son the forename Napoleone, which was prescient as it means "the lion of Naples". As Letizia later explained, "My uncle Napoleone died a few weeks before Ponte Novo, but he had come to Corsica to fight. It was in memory of this heroic man that I named my second son".

The child was born puny and sickly, but this only brought out his mother's maternal instincts more strongly. After an emergency baptism in his father's house, he was subsequently baptized two years later on 21 July 1771, in the cathedral of Ajaccio, by his great-uncle, Archdeacon Lucien. The ceremony was brief and very simple. His godfather was Lorenzo Giubeca, chief clerk to the Corsican States-General, and his godmother was his paternal aunt Gertruda Paravicini, who had been of great assistance at his birth and for whom Napoleon would always retain the greatest respect.

The certificate records that "in the year one thousand seven hundred and seventy-one, on the twenty-first of July, the sacraments and prayers were read over Napoléon, a son born of the legitimate marriage of M. Charles (son of Joseph Bonaparte) and the lady Marie Letizia, his wife, after he had been summarily baptized at his home, with the permission of the very reverend Lucien Buonaparte, having been born on the fifteenth of August one thousand seven hundred and sixty-nine."

*Left & below: Charles Bonaparte and Letizia's house, set in the heart of Ajaccio on the corner of rue Malerba (now rue Saint-Charles) and rue Pevero (now rue Letizia), was formerly the Bozzi residence but came into the couple's hands, after protracted wrangling, via a legacy in favour of Letizia. The house, modest in appearance but endowed with a typically Corsican charm, had three storeys, each with six windows, and it overlooked a small square. It was in the living room that the future Napoleon I first saw the light of day. Letizia brought up her children here until her exile to the mainland in 1793. On her return in 1796, she made several extensions to the house and carried out refurbishments. It is still standing today, having been donated to the French State in 1923 and turned into a French national museum devoted to Bonaparte in 1967.*

## Letizia Ramolino (1750–1836)

Doubts were expressed as to whether Letizia's husband Carlo was really the father of the young Napoleon, but the friendship linking Letizia with the Comte de Marbeuf should be understood as a desire to rise up the social scale. She was above all a woman of integrity, even if legend also represents her as extremely seductive. "Madame Mère" (this later became her title, a shortened form of Madame, the Mother of the Emperor) had a difficult life. She had to bring up her many children alone, cope with being expelled from Corsica in 1793 and settling near Toulon, survive the Revolution, and keep the whims and ambitions of her children under control. Under the Empire, her priority was to protect "the weakest". Her famous saying "long may it last" made her reputation as a prudent mother, and she lived up to it by welcoming her children to her home in Rome after the fall of Napoleon.

*Above: Tall and beautiful, Letizia was a woman of great character. Napoleon would later observe she was a "man's head on a woman's body. A woman from the Corsican mountains."*

Battesimo
Napoleone
Bona
Parte

L'anno mille settecento settant'uno à vent'uno Luglio si sono adempiate le sacre
Ceremonie e preci sopra di Napoleone figlio nato di legmo matrimonio
dal S.r Carlo Bonaparte de fù S.r Gius.e e dalla Sig.ra M.ra Letizia sua
moglie alquale gli fù data l'acqua in Casa dal M.to R.do Luciano Bonap.e
di Ricey.e nato li quindeci Agosto mille settecento sessanta nove
ed hanne assistito alle sacre Ceremonie per padrino S.r Ill.mo
Lorenzo Giubiga di Colej Procuratore del Re e per madrina la Sig.ra
M.ra Geltruda moglie del Sig.r Nicolò Paravicino. Presente
il P.re quali unitamente à me si sono sottoscritti
Gc.o Gratta Fiamande Ceonomo d'Ajaccio
                    Lorenzo Giubega        Geltruda Paravicini
Carlo Buonaparte

Battesimo
Maria
Anna
Bona
Parte

L'anno mille settecent settant'uno à vent'uno Luglio si sono adempiat
le sacre Ceremonie e preci sopra di M.ra Anna figlia nata di
legmo matrimonio dal S.r Carlo de fù S.r Gius.e Bonaparte
e dalla Sig.ra M.ra Letizia sua moglie nata quattordici
d.o ed hanno assistito alla sacre Ceremonie per pad.e S.r Ill.mo
Lorenzo Giubiga di Colej Procuratore del Re e per madrina
la Sig.ra Anna Peviano presente il P.re p.e di curiano
à me si sono sottoscritti Gc.o Gratta Fiamande Ceonomo
Carlo Buonaparte        Lorenzo Giubega        Anna Ferna

# Napoleon and Maria Anna Bonaparte's baptism certificate, 21 July 1771

Translation

### Baptism of Napoleon Bonaparte

In the year one thousand seventy-one, on the twenty-first of July, took place the sacred ceremonies and prayers in my presence, the Treasurer of Ajaccio, for Napoleon, son born of a legitimate marriage between Mr. Carlo Bonaparte, son of Giuseppe and Maria Letizia his spouse, who was born on the fifteen of August one thousand seven hundred sixty-nine. The following attended the sacred ceremonies and prayers, his godfather the Most Illustrious Lorenzo Giubega from Calvi, Representative of the King, and his godmother, Mrs. Geltruda, wife of Mr. Nicolò Paravisino, who together with me have signed this document.
Gio Batta Diamante, Treasurer of Ajaccio
Lorenzo Giubega
Geltrude Paravicina
Carlo Buonaparte

### Baptism of Maria Anna Bonaparte

In the year one thousand seventy-one, on the twenty-first of July, took place the sacred ceremonies and prayers for Maria Anna, daughter born of a legitimate marriage between Mr. Carlo Bonaparte, son of Giuseppe and Maria Letizia his spouse, who was born on the fourteen of July. The following attended the sacred ceremonies and prayers, her godfather the Most Illustrious Lorenzo Giubega from Calvi, Representative of the King, and her godmother, Mrs. Anna (?), who together with me have signed this document.
Gio Batta Diamante, Treasurer of Ajaccio
Lorenzo Giubega
Anna (?)
Carlo Buonaparte

# Youth

As a young boy, Napoleon was boisterous and impulsive, showing early signs of an extremely authoritarian and independent character. He was also a secretive child who liked to wander alone for hours. He sometimes sought refuge in a cave, still visible to this day, near the Casone monument. Napoleon's favourite toy was a small 30-pound (13.6-kilogram) cannon (still preserved in the Maison Bonaparte, now a museum). Because his father Carlo was often away from home on business, it was Letizia who ran the house and brought up her children with firm discipline, administering severe but fair punishments if necessary. In this way she instilled in Napoleon a sense of honour and keeping one's word, and of family loyalty, which he retained throughout his life.

Napoleon was first sent as a day pupil to a boarding school run by lay sisters, the Béguines d'Ajaccio, in a former Jesuit college. According to his mother's memoirs, he seems to have fallen for a young Giacominetta, which aroused "the jealousy of the other little girls". Incidentally, when he was mocked with the famous lines "Napoleone di mezza calzetta fa l'amore a Giacominetta" ("Napoleon with his stockings half off/Makes love to Giacominetta"), he is said to have taken revenge by giving some of his taunters a beating, a sign of his intransigent nature.

He was then placed in the class of the Abbé Recco, a family friend, who quickly recognized his abilities in arithmetic and reading. From this moment on, the boy could no longer tolerate mediocrity. "My temperament could not bear it, if I was not immediately top of the class," he later said.

He was unsociable by nature. His mother even recalled, "When he was eight, we had to build him a kind of small wooden room on the terrace of our house to which he would retreat for the whole day to avoid being bothered by his brothers."

Near Ajaccio, the family owned some land and salt works as well as the small Milelli estate. Among the fruit and olive trees Napoleon's youth seemed to be progressing smoothly, though he often played pranks which enraged his mother and grandmother. By now the Buonapartes had five children: Joseph, Napoleon, Lucien, Elisa and Louis. The time had come to secure their future.

Carlo, finally confirmed as being of noble rank and elected to the States-General in Versailles as the deputy for the nobility in June 1777, obtained a study bursary for each of his two elder sons. With the good will of the island's governor, the Comte de Marbeuf, the first two Buonaparte sons were sent to the mainland to complete their education at the seminary in Autun. Joseph was now destined for the priesthood and Napoleon for a military career. In December 1778 the two brothers and their father set sail for France. They would not see their mother again for seven years.

*Right: Napoleon was brought up mainly by his mother, Letizia. A strong-willed woman, she instilled strict principles in her children and supervised their education lovingly but unwaveringly. Throughout his life Napoleon would declare a boundless love for his mother, for whom he reserved all the honours of the Empire.*

**Above:** *Leaving Corsica with his brother Joseph, the young Bonaparte sets off for the mainland. He went first to the seminary in Autun where his father Charles had gone in December 1778.*

**Right:** *Napoleon only stayed at Autun for a few months; it was here that he learnt the French language. Coming from the Mediterranean, he found the climate very harsh.*

## Napoleon's brothers and sisters: Joseph (1768–1844), Lucien (1775–1840), Elisa (1777–1820), Louis (1778–1846), Pauline (1780–1825), Caroline (1782–1839), Jerome (1784–1860)

Lucien, a fierce republican who could never be persuaded to stay in line, stands apart from this imperial quartet of brothers. As President of the Council of Five Hundred, he played a crucial role in the coup d'état of Brumaire, but despite this he was sent away from Paris to be ambassador in Madrid (having briefly served as Minister of the Interior at the start of the Consulate). The quarrel with Napoleon continued until the Hundred Days (Napoleon's period in Paris after escape from Elba), particularly because of a marriage made without the emperor's consent, but the two brothers were reconciled in 1815. The other three brothers were largely associated with government. Joseph became King of Spain after wearing the crown of Naples; Louis (closest to Napoleon after spending his youth in Auxonne) took the throne of Holland; and Jerome, despite a brief escapade to the United States where he married an American woman, later reigned over Westphalia (his second wife was a German princess). The four brothers suffered varying fates after the end of the Empire.

Although Napoleon's sisters were too young to have spent much of their childhood close to him, they were at his side all through the Consulate and the Empire. Elisa became Princess of Piombino, then Grand Duchess of Tuscany and, with her husband Félix Bacciochi, was an active patron of Italian artists in Carrara. Caroline married Murat in 1800, became Queen of Naples and participated in public life in both France and Italy. Pauline, the Emperor's favourite, was married first to General Leclerc, who died on Saint-Domingue. She then married Prince Camillo Borghese, taking the title of Duchess of Guastalla. She set up home in Trianon, Neuilly and Florence, living up to her image which was synonymous with ease (her famous cures in Plombières) and sensuality (her body was immortalized in marble by the talented sculptor Canova). For a long time all three were opposed to the influence of Joséphine and the Beauharnais family, even to the extent of provoking their brother's rage at the moment of his coronation.

*Jerome* (**opposite**), *Lucien* (**above**) *and Pauline* (**left**) *had very different personalities but all played an important part in the life of their brother Napoleon. Jerome, the last surviving sibling, would witness the first years of the Second Empire and would pass on the baton to their nephew Napoleon III. Lucien, through his political commitments and, above all, his role as the President of the Council of the Five Hundred, succeeded in saving the situation on 18 Brumaire but did not flinch from making sacrifices for the benefit of his older brother. Finally, without Pauline's famous marble statue, it would be impossible to imagine her combination of "beauty and grace [for] there is no line in her body that one would wish to be different: she has limbs which, even seen in a mould, still attract lovers a hundred years after her death" (Frédéric Masson).*

# Brienne and the École Militaire

Together with Joseph, the young Napoleon arrived at Autun on 30 December 1778 and entered the seminary on 1 January 1779. He had barely had time to become familiar with the French language, having previously known only the rudiments, when he had to change schools. As the register shows, only three months and twenty days later he left the Jesuit School for the École Militaire in Brienne, which was under the protection of Cardinal de Loménie de Brienne. After taking the end of year examination, he was placed in the top class. In fact, his father had continued to pull strings in Paris and Versailles to get him a cadet bursary to one of the royal military academies.

Living in the small community of Brienne – about 18.5 miles (30 kilometres) from Troyes – Napoleon, with his strong Italian accent, was overcome by strong feelings of isolation. It must be said that the discipline of the Minim friars was exceptionally severe. Each pupil had only a modest cell containing just "a camp bed, a water jug and a washbasin". Meals were taken in a communal refectory seating eighty people, which can still be seen today. The food was sufficient to meet the pupils' basic needs and no more. For breakfast and supper they were given bread and seasonal fruits with water, and for lunch they had soup, a main course or a salad, and wine mixed with one-third water.

The pupils wore blue and red coats with white buttons, a blue jacket with a white lining and, depending on circumstances, blue or black breeches made of fine or coarse serge.

Napoleon took refuge in reading. He pushed himself so hard at his academic work that his teachers were full of admiration. He showed great aptitude for mathematics as well as history and geography.

He was not generally on good terms with his schoolfellows. He later said, "My schoolmates did not like me much". When asked his name, his reply, "Napolioné dé Buonaparté", spoken with a strong Corsican accent, attracted sarcastic comments and earned him the nickname "La paille au nez".

However, during the winter of 1783, his relationship with them changed completely. A heavy mantle of snow lay over the countryside of the Champagne region, completely covering the schoolyard. Inside the school the pupils became bored during their recreation periods. The young Corsican led his schoolfellows out for a legendary snowball fight, a real miniature war with trenches and pitched battles. The instigator, who

proved to be a real tactician and leader of men during this game, soon won the respect of all.

He kept up a copious correspondence with his family back in Corsica. He asked after his relatives and worried about their health and their futures. In the first of his letters to have been preserved, dated 25 June 1784, he talks of his brother Lucien who had joined him at Brienne: "He is in the second class for Latin, and will be learning all the different parts of the curriculum. He shows a lot of aptitude and willingness. It is to be hoped that this will be a good subject. He is in good health, plump, bright and careless, and so far they are pleased with him. He speaks French very well and has completely forgotten Italy."

After achieving a brilliant result in the competitive entrance examination and obtaining the necessary age dispensation, Napoleon was admitted to the École Militaire in Paris and swiftly moved to the royal capital. He entered on 19 October 1784. This academy, founded by Louis XV and located on the Champ de Mars, took in the best pupils from the twelve provincial royal military academies. As soon as they were admitted to this establishment, the pupils were given the title of "cadet-gentilhomme". Napoleon was in the artillery and naval section. He later chose the artillery, as his mother begged him not to go off sailing the seas.

At the age of fifteen, Bonaparte had become much less reserved and made friends more easily with his fellow pupils. He proved to be kind and generous and ready to sacrifice himself for those in need. One of his essays shows evidence of this:

"To find happiness yourself, you must work for the happiness

**Right & far right:** *Concerned about his future, the young Napoleon was a diligent student, particularly in Brienne. Devoting many hours to his studies, he was a voracious reader and often spent part of his recreation periods in the library rather than playing with his companions. Very early on he showed a great aptitude for mathematics and a passion for both history and geography. His poor French and strong Corsican accent made him the frequent butt of jokes. Legend has it that Napoleon only won acceptance after an intense snowball fight in which he proved himself a peerless leader.*

## Louis-Antoine Fauvelet de Bourrienne (1769–1834)

Bourrienne and Bonaparte were born in the same year. They met as boys in Brienne and quickly became friends. However, they parted ways on the eve of the Revolution, when Bourrienne chose the diplomatic service. It was not until 1797, at the time of the Treaty of Leoben with Austria, that Bonaparte remembered his former friend and chose him for his secretary. Bourrienne continued in this post for the next few years, holding it during the Consulate, but after being compromised in a shady affair in 1802, he was dismissed and became chargé d'affaires in Hamburg. His *Mémoires*, which run to ten volumes, are without doubt one of the most important sources of information on Napoleon's youth.

**Above:** *During the five-year spell in Brienne, two youngsters became close friends. Although very different, they shared a mutual admiration and invariably supported each other. While Bourrienne assisted Napoleon with his Latin, the latter helped his friend solve mathematical problems.*

of others. What joy to die surrounded by children and to be able to say: I secured the happiness of hundreds of families; I had a hard and difficult life, but the nation will benefit from my work: I have had troubles, my friends have had serenity; I have been worried, they have been happy; I have had the pain and they have had the joys."

The school, which had been visited in May by the Maréchal de Ségur, allowed its pupils to make free use of their time. They had to be present for four hours of study, two in the morning and two in the evening, during which they "wrote their letters, read the classics or took lessons in English or calligraphy". Shooting practice and horse-riding were also part of the curriculum.

Napoleon left the academy, having passed the final examination after only ten months' teaching (instead of the normal two years). His position, forty-second out of fifty-eight, is praiseworthy considering his special circumstances – he had learned of the death of his father in Montpellier in February 1785. From this time on, Napoleon alone would be responsible for meeting the needs of his entire family.

**Above:** *While his classmates in the École Militaire were thinking of following the route mapped out for them, Bonaparte was already dreaming about a great future career.*

**Bottom:** *In October 1784, Napoleon entered the École Militaire, situated on the edge of the Champ de Mars in Paris. Here he learned the principles of leadership, as well as fencing and horse riding.*

**Below:** *Mathematics and geography captured the imagination of Bonaparte, and he would treasure his first compass for many years afterwards.*

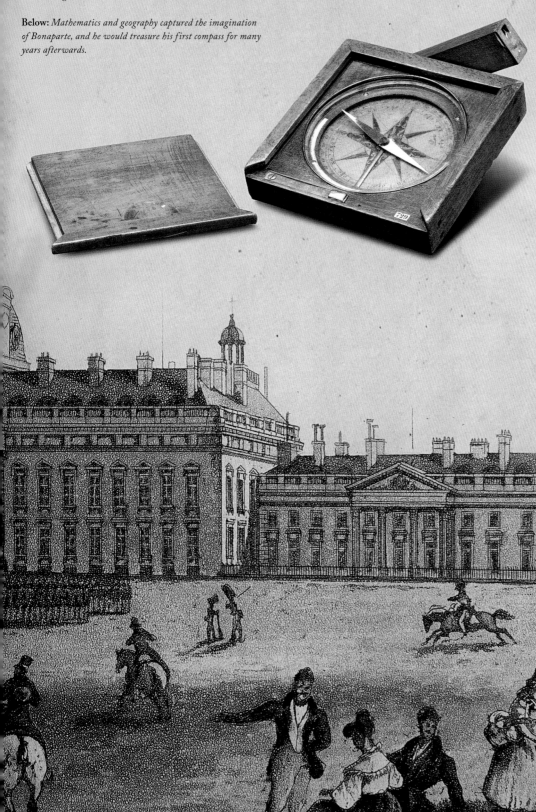

Marbeuf came to prominence at the Battle of Ponte Novo but is mainly remembered for his alleged liaison with Letizia. In reality, this son of a great Breton nobleman who had replaced Chauvelin and then the Comte de Vaux as the head of the French army in Corsica, was a scrupulous governor. He had been Condé's colonel of dragoons.

**Above:** *As the protector of Charles Bonaparte and his family, Marbeuf laid himself open to unfounded allegations of an affair with Letizia, and even to rumours that he was Napoleon's father.*

## Letter from Napoleon to his cousin, December 1784

Of all Bonaparte's early letters, this one from December 1784 is one of the most interesting. He is writing to his cousin, Arigghi di Casanova, from the military school in Paris and outlines his schedule, so that Arigghi can come and see him, as he himself cannot leave. After also thanking his cousin for helping him obtain a place, he signs off as "Napoleone di Buonaparte".

9 heure ... ou a 4 heures. ou jeudi
a 9. 10. 11 heures vous devez savoir
que je vous marque les heures parceque
nous ne somme libre que dans ces
ins tants et dans tout autre temps
~~vous~~ je ne pourai avoir l'honneur
et le plaisir de vous embrasser
je vous prie cependent si vos affaires
vous le permette de venir mecredi
ou jeudi. adieu mon cher cousin je
voudrai bien avoir la liberté
de sortir je serai deja venu vous
assurer de mes respects et de ma
reconnoisence.
Napoleone di
Buonaparte

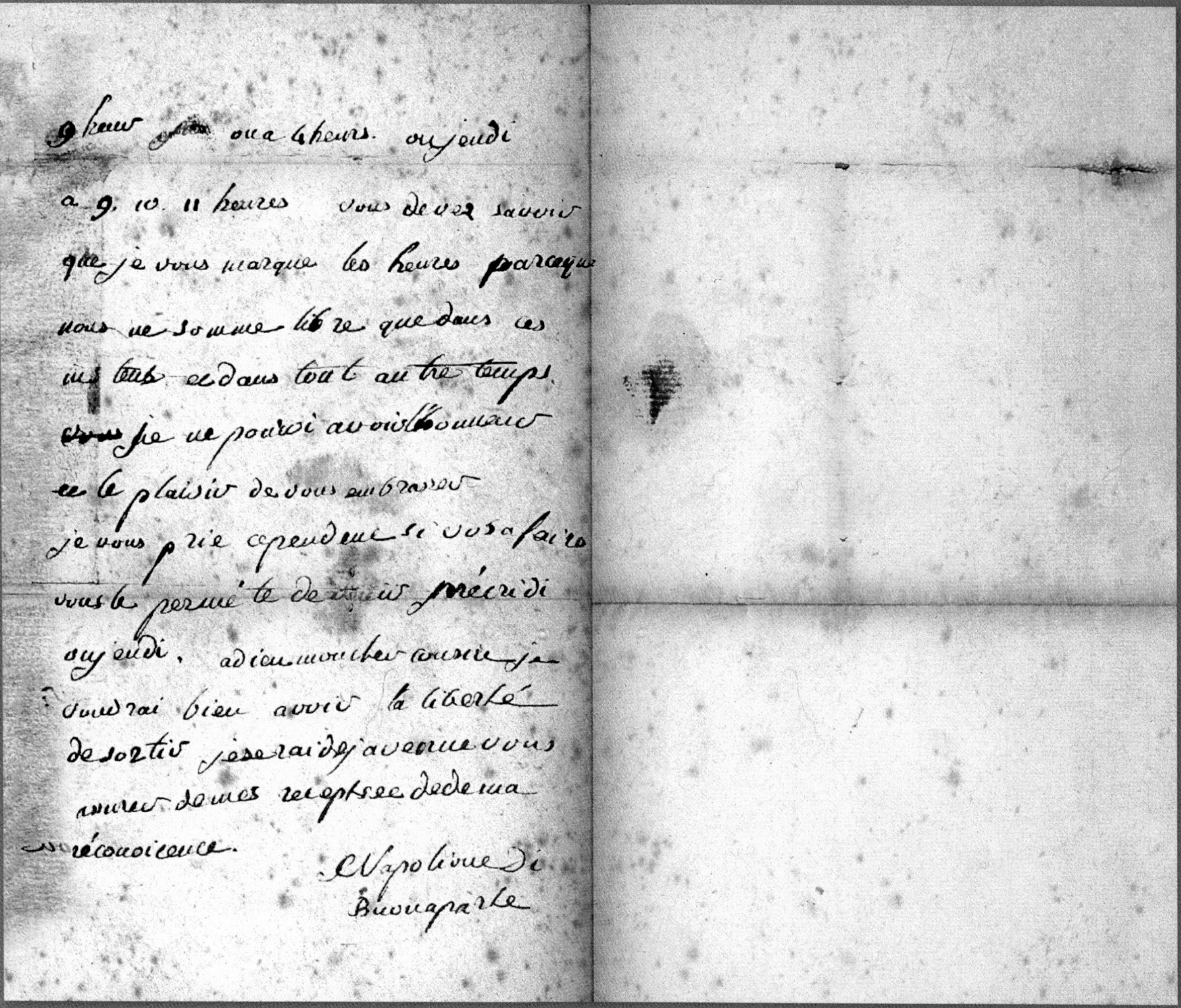

**Translation**

To Monsieur
Monsieur Arigo ( ?) di Casa Neuva ( ?)
… at the Hotel de Provence rue cimetière st andré des arts …

If Monsieur de Casa is curious to see one of his fellow countrymen, one of his relatives, in a word someone who is fond of him, he only has to trouble himself to come to the Royal Military School [one word smudged and illegible] this is where he will find his most humble and most affectionate (?) servant Bonaparte who will thank him face to face for his efforts in … and much else besides. He is urged to do so at the earliest and to come on Wednesday or Friday, or Saturday, or Monday from 9 O' clock… or at 4 O'clock. Or Thursday at 9, 10, 11 O'clock. You must know that I specify times because we are free only during these… and at all other times you (word crossed out in the text) I would not be able to have the honour and the pleasure to embrace you. I beg you however if business affairs allow to come on Wednesday or Thursday. Farewell my dear cousin, I would love to be free to go out. I would already have come to assure you of my respects and of my gratitude.

Napoleone Di
Buonaparte

# Early Career

In Valence, Napoleon learned that he had been assigned to the La Fère artillery regiment. He was to serve in Captain Masson d'Auterive's company of bombardiers. As always, Napoleon lived slightly apart from his comrades. He lodged with Mademoiselle Bou, and used his rare moments of leisure to read. His landlady, the owner of the Café-Cercle, lived next door to the Pierre-Marc Aurel bookshop, where Bonaparte obtained, usually in the form of loans, the works of Rousseau.

He was now writing his first essays, most notably an essay on Corsica – his now famous "Réfutation de Roustan", in which he defended Rousseau – and on suicide. He really seems to have felt separated by a deep gulf in the matter of moral standards and attitudes. This sense of ill-being conveys his despair in the face of "his situation as a poor junior officer, without protection, who, despite his noble blood, would not find it easy to enter the higher ranks", and was not helped by being so far away from his family, whom he had left seven years previously: "While I am in the first flush of my youth, I can still hope to live for a long time. I have been absent from my homeland for six or seven years. How delightful it would be to see my compatriots and my parents again in four months' time!"

It was in Valence that he learned how to be a soldier and became an officer. His first exercises in the field were a revelation to him. When his friend des Mazis reproached him for not having much fun, he responded with the verse: "Plus l'esprit est fort, plus il faut qu'il agisse; il meurt dans le repos, il vit dans l'exercice" which translates as "The stronger the spirit, the more it needs to act; it dies at rest, it lives in exercise". He read treatises on the art of warfare as well as the great philosophers (Rousseau, Voltaire, Montesquieu) and the great political thinkers (Mirabeau, Necker) of his time. However, the financial situation of the future emperor was far from comfortable as he was using most of his meagre pay to support his brothers and sisters in Corsica. Yet it was while he was in Valence that he is said to have had an affair with Caroline, the young daughter of Madame Grégoire du Colombier.

After returning to Corsica for a brief stay, he set off for Toulon and Paris to try to obtain payment of compensation owed to his family by the government following the planting of mulberry trees at the Salines d'Ajaccio. In Paris, he stayed at the Hôtel de Cherbourg where, during any time he had to spare, he wrote numerous articles notable for showing his republican sentiments: "Kings make war for their personal glory, republics fight to defend the freedom of their citizens." Or: "I only

**Opposite below left:** *Jean-Jacques Rousseau was one of the young Bonaparte's early influences but other authors, such as the Abbé Raynal and Volney, attracted his attention in the first years of the Revolution.*

**Right:** *The storming of the Bastille was a symbol of the early revolutionary period but it also represented a major landmark for a whole generation of officers and students in the royal schools. Three years after this event of 14 July 1789, French troops began almost a quarter of a century of battles against an alliance of European monarchies.*

**Below:** *Social customs and standards were turned upside down. The demise of the Ancien Régime ushered in new attitudes to both male and female clothing as part of the drive to celebrate new liberties.*

express the truth, I feel I have the strength to tell it." He also worked at mathematics and invented a geometrical theorem that is still known as Napoleon's Theorem: "The centres of the three equilateral triangles constructed on the exterior of each of the three sides of any triangle form an equilateral triangle."

In Paris, on 22 November 1787, he lost his virginity to a young prostitute from the Palais Royal. The palace, which had been sacked after the departure of Philippe-Égalité, had become a place where people met under its crowded galleries. At all hours of the day and night, shopkeepers, café owners and young women of loose morals attracted the curious passers-by.

It was in order to rejoin the La Fère regiment that Bonaparte first went to Auxonne. Under the command of Baron Du Teil, he underwent rigorous training. The military manoeuvres took place on the polygone d'artillerie, a few hundred metres from the centre of town. When he had a little time to spare, as well as reading he often went on long walks or played lotto. Despite his very full timetable, he was also supervising the education of his young brother Louis who was with him at the time. On 19 and 20 July 1789, five days after the storming of the Bastille, it was in Auxonne that he witnessed his first revolutionary riot, and then the revolt by the gunners of his regiment. He swore an oath of loyalty to the Nation, the King and the Law in the Place des Casernes in Auxonne. And after the night of 4 August he wrote, "This year augurs well for honest folk, after so many centuries of oppression and slavery."

On 14 July 1790, on his return to Valence for the Fête de la Fédération celebrating the establishment of a constitutional monarchy, Napoleon swore an oath. In August of the same year, he celebrated the Fête du Roi with friends.

On 10 July 1792, he was promoted to captain. One month later to the day, on 10 August, he witnessed the massacre of the Swiss Guards outside the Tuileries, followed by the departure of Louis XVI. These terrible scenes haunted him for a long time and filled him with a certain distrust of Parisians for the rest of his life.

In 1793, he learned of the governing National Convention's decision to force Paoli's supporters to return to French rule. An uprising was inevitable. Surrounded by faithful friends whom he had won over to his cause, Napoleon hoped to reconquer his native city. But on 23 May, just as he was leaving Saint-Florent, the Casa Bonaparte was sacked by his political adversaries. Arriving at Ajaccio, he took refuge for three days in the tower of Capitello, but was forced to retreat along the road to Porticcio. He then had to ride on horseback to Calvi to join the rest of his family who were already in safety. Exile became inevitable and they decided to leave for the mainland, finally departing on 11 June 1793.

**Left:** *To mark the first anniversary of the storming of the Bastille, the Festival of the Federation gathered together all the deputies from the 83 French départements around Louis XVI. This gathering of over 400,000 people was both populist and highly symbolic; from 1880, 14 July would be commemorated as a national holiday.*

**Right:** *All the constituent parts of the State united around the flag in a spirit of national harmony. These aspirations were very quickly shattered, however.*

**Below:** *The storming of the Tuileries on 10 August 1792 threatened the power of the monarchy. The mob seized the palace despite the resistance of the Swiss Guard protecting the Royal Family; the radicalization of the movement became unstoppable.*

# Pasquale Paoli (1725–1807)

Paoli exercised such fascination over the young Napoleon that for a long time he was unable to imagine that his destiny lay anywhere other than Corsica. Probably because Paoli spent so much time in exile, he became a legendary figure for Bonaparte. After his appointment as general-in-chief in 1755, Paoli was the first to attempt an experiment with democracy in Corsica, causing Rousseau to write in *Du Contrat Social*: "There is still one land in Europe that is capable of legislation: that is the island of Corsica. The bravery and constancy with which these good people have succeeded in recovering and defending their liberty deserve to have some wise man teach them how to preserve it. I have a premonition that one day this little island will astound Europe." After Ponte Novo, Paoli lived in exile for almost twenty years, and though his return was greeted with joy, it turned into a nightmare for several of his fervent admirers. The many pacts he made with the English who finally deposed him, coupled with the downfall of his democratic system, forced him into a final exile. Before Paoli's death in 1807, Napoleon rejected the former Corsican general's offers to serve him.

# The Siege of Toulon

The Buonaparte family moved into the rue Lafon in Marseille. Then from June 1793 they took up residence in Toulon, more precisely in the little village of La Valette. A brief stop at Beaucaire on 28 July of the same year inspired Napoleon to write his only great political essay, the famous "Souper" ("The Supper"), in which he presents an exciting confrontation through an unlikely encounter between the adversaries of the time. In this essay – page by page and just beneath the surface – we discover some federalist leanings, with a call for republicanism and the support of the National Convention.

In Corsica, he had already joined the battle against Sardinia at La Maddalena. Paoli had entrusted this diversion to his nephew, Colonel Colonna Cesari, who had 600 men under his command, including a very modest artillery section, already under the orders of the young Napoleon. Napoleon's assignment had been to seize the small island of San Stefano, separated from La Maddalena by a narrow channel. With about fifty men, he had captured the Sardinian defenders and landed his artillery.

Now, in September 1793, Napoleon's compatriot Saliceti entrusted him with the command of the artillery section of the troops at Toulon after the commander was wounded. Napoleon was quick to act. The English and Spanish (supporting royalist French forces) had set up camp outside the city, taken command of the French port and were thumbing their noses at the Republic. Via La Ciotat on 5 September, then Ollioules two days later, Napoleon joined the National Convention troops commanded by General Carteaux who was besieging the city but had failed to recapture it. His proposals were intriguing. With only four cannons and two mortars, his intention was to drive back the enemy and force them to abandon their positions. He was rapidly promoted to the rank of major, and his powers of persuasion finally won over even the most hesitant. Reinforcements arrived with Dugommier

## Jean-Andoche Junot (1771–1813)

There was more to "La tempête" (the storm), as he was nicknamed by his friends, than just the feats of arms that punctuated his life: the cannonball that left him unafraid at Toulon, the victory over the Turks at Nazareth in 1799, Saragossa in 1808, and the battle of Valoutina. He was the faithful companion, the constant friend, who did not hesitate to share Napoleon's fate at the trickiest moments. And when the wheel turned in their favour, his good fortune was simply the result of his own courage. He was rewarded with the posts of governor of Paris, ambassador and then governor in Portugal, before he finally came to grief in the madness at Ragusa, where he held the post of Governor of the Illyrian Provinces. Despite his unfaithfulness to his wife, Laure Permon, she defended his memory in her *Souvenirs*, a publication which is still a classic of Napoleonic literature, despite its inaccuracies and distortion of the truth.

**Above & below:** *The Siege of Toulon revealed Bonaparte's qualities as a military strategist when he took the city after a sustained assault. The young officer's obstinacy ensured the success of his plan to first capture the Éguillette fort in order to be able to bombard the English ships in the harbour.*

who took over command on 16 November. The action against the British General O'Hara's men quickly proved decisive and O'Hara was taken prisoner.

For Doppet, who had briefly succeeded Carteaux, all Napoleon's genius was revealed in that moment: "This young officer was not only extremely talented but also unusually bold and untiringly active. During all the inspections I made of this army, I always found him at his post; if he needed a moment's rest, he would lie on the ground wrapped in a coat; he never left his batteries."

After leaving the village of La Seyne on 17 December, Napoleon led the decisive attack on "Little Gibraltar" and the Éguillette fort. Sergeant Junot, who was at his side and was to remain with him for the rest of his life, had just enough time to write on a sign in front of the cannons, "Battery of the fearless men", before grapeshot began to rain down on the soldiers. However, their commander remained unmoved. As the French columns advanced, he sent around 8,000 bombs into Fort Mulgrave, which was forced to surrender. The fall of Fort Malbousquet put an end to hostilities.

The English and Spanish were forced to retreat and their fleets left Toulon the next day. Napoleon entered the city two days later. It was here in Toulon, on 22 December, that he became a brigadier-general, a promotion that was confirmed on 6 February the following year. He was twenty-four years old.

**Above & opposite:** *Taking the Éguillette fort was no easy feat. After the enemy positions were bombarded the soldiers engaged in ferocious hand-to-hand fighting.*

**Below:** *This map of the Siege of Toulon shows that Bonaparte's choice of pressure points proved crucial. The operation he initiated led to the domination of both the city and enemy positions. A French victory was inevitable.*

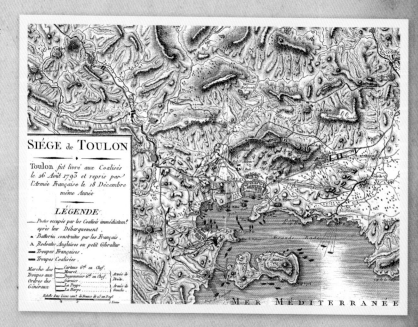

que je me suis donné pour former promptement l'Équipage de Siège
Voyez la feuille cotée **A**.

Il y a plus d'un mois que j'ai dit aux généraux que l'artillerie existante dans ce moment ci étoit plus le cas d'éteindre le feu de la Redoute anglaise placée sur le sommet du promontoire de l'aiguillette nous devons donc distinguer deux périodes différentes dans le siège de Toulon.

Première période. La prise de l'aiguillette, l'expulsion des anglais de la Rade, et le Bombardement de d'ambemême tous presque partout

Effet que doit produire cette première attaque

nous rendre maître de Toulon par la commotion générale que cela peut produire, et par la crainte de tomber dans nos mains, et de ne pouvoir exécuter la Retraite

Travaux qu'il faut faire pour cet objet

Batterie du Sans culotte                                        Existante

| 1 Couleuvrine de 64. | Située au fond de la rade de la pointe du Brégaillon |
| 2 Pièce de 36. | elle a fait son effet a chassé tous |
| 3 Pièce de 24 | les pontons Bombardes et frégates qui |
| 2 mortier marin | se tenoient sur la gauche de l'aiguillette |

Batterie du Bréguat                                            Existante

| 1 Pièce de 36. | elle Balaye la rive de la droite de |
| 2 Pièce de 24. | l'aiguillette et toute cette partie de |
| 1 mortier marin | la grande Rade |

Batterie de la grande Rade                                     Existante

| 2 Pièce de 24 | elle fait le même effet que celle du Bréguat les 2 Batteries ont déjà fait leur effet elles ont chassé les Pontons et Bombardes qui étoient a la droite de l'aiguillette |

Batterie du Sabletter                                          Existante

| 4 Pièce de 24 | dirigé sur une Batterie l'aiguillette la Redoute anglaise dite de l'aiguillette |
| 3 mortier de 12 po |

## Plan for the Siege of Toulon, 1793

Manuscript of the plan for the Siege of Toulon, drawn up by the aide-de-camp Junot but dictated and annotated by Bonaparte. The young officer was already showing himself to be the peerless strategist who would go on to become Emperor.

**Translation**

More than a month ago I told the generals that the existing artillery at the time was not up to wiping out the fire of the English redoubt positioned on the summit of the headland of laiguillette.

We must therefore distinguish two different phases in the Siege of Toulon.

First phase. The capture of laiguillette, the expulsion of the English from the natural harbours , and the shelling.  At the same time (?) to attack Maraude (?).

Expected result of this first phase

To give us mastery of Toulon through the resulting general upheaval, and through [spreading] the fear of falling into our hands, without being able to retreat.

Work to be done to achieve these objectives

**The Sans Culotte Battery**      Already in place

|  |  |
|---|---|
| 1 (?) of 44 | Situated at the edge of the sea on the |
| 2 pieces of 36 | Braigaillon promontory it has achieved |
| 3 pieces of 24 | the desired effect to drive away all the |
| 2 marine mortars | pontoons bomb-ships and frigates which |
|  | were on the left-hand side of l'Aiguillette. |

**The Breguat Battery**      Already in place

|  |  |
|---|---|
| 1 pieces of 36 | It overlooks the shore to the right of |
| 2 pieces of 24 | Laiguillette and the whole of this side |
| 1 marine mortar | of la Grande Rade. |

**The Grande Rade Battery**      Already in place

|  |  |
|---|---|
| 2 pieces of 24 | It had the same effect as the one on the |
|  | Breguat these two batteries have already |
|  | produced some result by driving away the |
|  | pontoons and bomb-ships which were |
|  | on the right of laiguillette. |

**The Sablettes Battery**      Already in place

|  |  |
|---|---|
| 4 pieces of 24 | Sited on a height above (?) the English |
| 3 mortars of 12 | redoubt so-called l'aiguillette. |
| [one illegible | |
| abbreviation] | |

# Crossing the Desert

After many return trips between Marseille and Toulon for tours of inspection, Napoleon was appointed commander of artillery for the army of Italy on 7 February 1794. His first travels took him to Saint-Tropez, Nice and then Menton. He was getting the measure of his new assignment and even went to the Col de Tende in order to think out a possible route for his troops. He joined his family for a few days at the Château-Sallé, a villa which they had moved into shortly before. But very soon his new duties and plans of attack took him to Nice where he lodged for a few days. Then, on 20 and 21 May, he went to Colmar with Augustin Robespierre. Brother of "the Incorruptible" Maximilien, he was a leading figure in the government during the Reign of Terror with whom Napoleon was on friendly terms, and whose convictions he appeared to share.

It was in July, at the camp in Siege, that Napoleon learned of the events of Thermidor in 1794 and Robespierre's fall from power. Suspected of active collaboration with the regime of Terror, Bonaparte was arrested in Nice on 9 August. The next day he was imprisoned in Fort Carré in Antibes, where he remained until 20 August.

Napleon accepted his misfortune with patience, waiting for events to turn in his favour. Although he was soon freed, the young victor of Toulon could no longer count on any support from central powers. Having been one of the closest friends of Maximilien's brother, he had lost his influence.

It was then that Napoleon and his brother Joseph made the acquaintance of the Clary sisters, the daughters of a Marseille merchant. The younger, Désirée, was eight years younger than Napoleon. In her memoirs, she recalls, "We had not known him [Napoleon] for long when he said to us, 'in a good relationship, one of the two has to give way to the other. You, Joseph, have an indecisive nature, and Désirée is the same, whereas Julie and I know what we want. So you would do better to marry Julie. As for Désirée, she will be my wife.'" Désirée, who was still very naive, succumbed to the charms of Napoleon, whom she considered "a fine fellow, noisily cheerful and altogether a nice lad". But the two young people had to wait until 21 April 1795 before becoming engaged as Désirée's mother was rather reluctant to give her consent, saying, "One Bonaparte in the family is enough for me!", as Joseph had married Julie in the meantime.

On 15 June 1795 Napoleon was appointed brigadier-general of the infantry in the Army of the West, but in protest at what he considered a distasteful position he took sick leave and stayed on in Paris. Laure Permon, Duchess of Abrantès and the future wife of Junot, knew him well and described the young man in a state of utter poverty:

"At this time, Napoleon was so ugly and took so little care of his appearance that his unkempt, unpowdered hair made him unpleasant to look at. I can still see him coming into the courtyard of the Hôtel de la Tranquillité, crossing it with clumsy, uncertain steps, wearing a nasty round hat pulled down over his eyes, from

**Above:** *Bonaparte's close relationship with Robespierre's brother Augustin not only put him under suspicion but also stirred animosity amongst colleagues unsympathetic with his political forthrightness.*

**Right:** *In Marseille, Bonaparte met the Clary family, which entrenched him still further within the French bourgeoisie.*

which two long 'oreilles de chien' tresses of hair escaped and hung down over his redingote [greatcoat], his long, thin, black hands, without gloves because, he said, it was a needless expense, wearing badly made boots, and the generally sickly look resulting from his thinness and sallow complexion."

Who could have imagined that in less than five years Napoleon would become Premier Consul? His only interest was in literature and he dreamed of becoming a writer. At this time, he sketched out a novel, *Clisson et Eugénie*, whose two main characters are generally believed to have been inspired by his relationship with Désirée Clary. When their passion died, he wrote, "Farewell, you whom I had chosen as the arbiter of my life, farewell, companion of my finest days! In your arms, I have tasted supreme happiness. I had exhausted life and its worldly goods. What was left to me in future but satiety and boredom? At twenty-six, I have exhausted the transitory pleasures of reputation, but in your love, I tasted the sweet emotion of man's life."

On 18 August, he was attached to the topographical bureau of the Committee of Public Safety. However, his role as tactical adviser to the Armies of the Republic appeared subordinate to the decision-makers crowding in from all sides. On 15 September, he was first relieved of his office and then commissioned to lead troops in Turkey. But on the 24th, royalist agitation led by the Parisian sections against the proclamation of the results of a referendum on the constitution of year III – whose decrees would give two-thirds of the National Convention re-election – descended upon the streets. Director Paul Barras, remembering the brilliant success of the young artilleryman of Toulon, called on Napoleon to put down the insurrection.

**Above:** *From 9 to 20 August 1794, Bonaparte was imprisoned as a Robespierriste in the fort of Carré d'Antibes: On his release, he decided to go to Paris in order to consolidate his career. He was destined to rise once again.*

**Right:** *Laure Permon, wife of General Junot and a close friend of Napoleon whom he nicknamed "Petite Peste".*

## Désirée Clary (1777–1860)

Before he became the glorious general of his first campaigns, Napoleon had settled in the south of France with his family. It was during a stay in Marseille that he and his brother Joseph met the Clary sisters. The elder, Julie, married his brother, while he became engaged to the younger sister, Désirée. But after the first passionate letters, his move away to Paris put an end to this youthful love affair. However, the young lady was to have a fairytale destiny (made famous in film). By marrying General Bernadotte, she later became Queen of Sweden. Her descendants were the foundation of the current Swedish dynasty.

**Above & left:** *Désirée Clary married Jean Baptiste Jules Bernadotte, but would never forget the feelings stirred within her by her former fiancé Bonaparte. She offered him loyal friendship right up to the last years of the Empire.*

# Vendémiaire

The political situation continued to deteriorate. Born amid the debris of the Thermidorian Reaction, the Directory had to confront a large number of threats and conspiracies. In October 1795 several sections rejected the additional laws of the new constitution and one of them, the Lepelletier section, met at the Convent of the Filles Saint-Thomas and gave the signal to begin an uprising.

Appointed to lead the government troops to put down the royalist uprising, Napoleon succeeded in forcing the demonstrators to retreat. He did not hesitate to shoot in front of the steps of the Church of Saint Roch, impressing people as much by his calm and rigour as by the clinical way in which he carried out his mission. However, he benefited from the fiery spirit of an intrepid young cavalryman, Joachim Murat, a Gascon from the Lot region. Thanks to his actions, the forty

cannons of the Camp des Sablons were carried off and swiftly transported to the field of battle. The paths of the two men would not diverge for more than twenty years.

*The Memorial of Saint Helena* by Las Cases tells the story of the event in some detail:

"The Convention was in a state of extreme agitation. To clear themselves of blame, the representatives of the army hastily accused [General] Menou, attributing to treason what had only resulted from a lack of ability. ... Napoleon who had heard everything and knew what was going on, pondered for about half an hour on what he had to do. War to the death was breaking out between the Convention and Paris. Would it be a wise move to declare oneself, to speak in the name of the whole of France? Who would dare to descend alone into the arena to make himself the champion of the Convention? "Even

**Below & right:** *The popular legend and iconography resulting from the battle with the royalists entrenched inside the Church of Saint Roch, the culmination of 13 Vendémiaire, made Bonaparte a republican hero and the artillery the key military force.*

## Paul François Jean Nicolas, Vicomte de Barras (1755–1829)

Originally from Provence, Barras served in India before returning to his native land in 1789. The département of Var sent him to the Convention as a deputy where he voted for the execution of Louis XVI. He met Bonaparte in Toulon, and remembered him in 1795 on the occasion of 13 Vendémiaire. But when Bonaparte returned from Egypt, Barras ceded power to the new conqueror.

**Above:** *Barras played a crucial role in furthering the young Bonaparte's early career, not least by urging him to take on new responsibilities and by guiding him into the capital's political circles.*

victory would have something odious about it, whereas defeat would incur for ever the loathing of future races. How could one sacrifice oneself in this way to be the scapegoat for so many crimes for which one was not responsible? Why voluntarily lay oneself open to swelling, within a few brief hours, the ranks of those whose names are only spoken with loathing? But on the other hand, if the Convention succumbs, what will become of the great truths of our Revolution? Our many victories, the blood so often shed, will be no more than shameful actions. The foreigner, whom we have beaten so many times, will triumph and heap scorn upon us … Thus the defeat of the Convention would crown a foreign head and set the seal on the shame and slavery of the fatherland. … Napoleon positioned his artillery at the head of the Pont Louis XVI, the Pont-Royal, the rue de Rohan, the Cul-de-sac Dauphin, in the rue Saint-Honoré, at the Pont-Tournant etc; he entrusted the guarding to reliable officers. The fuse was lit everywhere and the little army sent to various posts or held in reserve in the gardens or at the Carrousel. The call to arms was sounded throughout Paris and the national guards formed up at all the entrances, surrounding the palace and the gardens. Their drummers made so bold as to come and sound the call to arms at the Carrousel and in the Place Louis XV."

At the conclusion of this episode – which would become known as 13 Vendémiaire – Napoleon was appointed general-in-chief of the Army of the Interior. His career had been launched. From this moment on nothing could stand in the way of his rise, particularly as he had made the acquaintance of a young widow, Marie-Joseph Rose Tascher de la Pagerie. He fell in love with her and, from then on, would always call her Joséphine.

*Opposite & below: Giving orders all the while, Napoleon confidently rode towards the insurgents retreating up the steps of the Church of Saint Roch. He had acquired the stature of a leader. Despite the drama of the situation, this print by Raffet shows the new French military chief as unruffled and sure of his authority. The legend had been forged.*

## Joachim Murat (1767–1815)

Fiery, intrepid and courageous, Joachim Murat was for a long time Napoleon's lucky star. In Vendémiaire, this innkeeper's son from the Lot region succeeded in seizing the cannons of the Sablons reserve to win the day. At Aboukir, he turned a site that had been associated with a naval defeat into a victory. In Brumaire, he fired the soldiers with enthusiasm and convinced them they should evict the deputies from the Council of Saint-Cloud. Marshal Murat, who played a decisive role at Austerlitz, Eylau and in Prussia, had long dreamed of wearing the crown of Spain though Napoleon eventually handed him the crown of Naples. As a king, he was loved by his subjects, put an end to feudalism and had a happy marriage with Caroline Bonaparte. He was also a great help to his brother-in-law in the snows of Russia. However, he did not take part in the last campaigns (France in 1814 and Belgium in 1815), because he was trying at all costs to preserve his power in Italy against the Austrians. His career ended at Pizzo, where he was executed after a last ditch stand.

# Marriage to Joséphine

It was in September 1795, in the circles that formed around the Director Barras, that Napoleon first met Joséphine. She was thirty-two and he was twenty-six. She was a woman of character, seductive and full of spirit. She already had plenty of experience of life. Born of an aristocratic family of planters based in Martinique, she was sent to Paris in 1779. There she married the Vicomte de Beauharnais, with whom she had two children, Eugène and Hortense. The ill-matched couple soon separated. In 1794, they were reunited by the Terror, when they were both imprisoned in the former Carmelite convent. Joséphine alone escaped the guillotine and was freed on 6 August after three months' detention. Far from being discouraged, she became one of the great personalities of Paris, organizing soirées and dinners to which the cream of the new Republic were invited, including her friend Madame Tallien. Napoleon immediately fell under her spell, dazzled by how at ease she was in public. She found it amusing, but succumbed, flattered by so much unbridled passion. The letters written to her by the young Corsican were passionate: "Your portrait and the intoxicating party yesterday evening have left my senses no peace …".

Napoleon's future appeared auspicious, especially as he soon saw the advantages to be gained from marrying this aristocratic lady who could open all the doors necessary for his future success. Napoleon later said that Barras himself had advised him to enter this union with Joséphine, one that would rid him of his Corsican name and make him completely French.

So he asked for Joséphine's hand, and she accepted out of love, though she was also urged on by her son Eugène who had already been promoted to aide-de-camp by her future father-in-law. The banns were published on 7 February 1796. Joséphine provided an attested affidavit, which meant she did not have to produce her certificate of baptism. The civil wedding was celebrated on 9 March (19 Ventôse, year IV of the Republican calendar). On the previous day they had signed a marriage

*Below: Joséphine was born in Trois-Îlets on Martinique, from where she would go on to fulfil a fabulous destiny, greater than that of any queen.*

Above: *Joséphine's marriage in March 1796 to "Puss-in-Boots" (her nickname for Bonaparte) would radically change her life. In their house on rue Chantereine, quickly renamed Victoire to extol the glory of her illustrious husband, she adopted a bourgeois lifestyle that would bring with it many friendships.*

## Marie-Joseph Rose Tascher de la Pagerie (1763–1814)

Born in Martinique, this young woman was the muse of the Directory and Barras. The start of her liaison with Bonaparte can be dated to 28 October 1795. The following year, she took Napoleon as her second husband. Their passionate correspondence is considered a model of its kind. She admired and feared him while he loved the woman he nicknamed Joséphine and handed almost everything over to her. Following infidelity on both sides, their reconciliation on Napoleon's return from Egypt enabled Joséphine to buy the property of Malmaison, to have access to the Tuileries and to be fully associated with his reign. She was crowned in Notre-Dame, but later had to settle for divorce in 1810. Nevertheless, she kept her title of Empress and her "maison", as well as receiving a generous pension until her death in 1814. Her unusual career seems to have borne out the prediction that an old servant woman in Martinique is said to have made when Joséphine was a child: "Dear little mistress, me see in the cloud big condor fly very high with rose in its beak ... You be Rose ... You, very unhappy ... then you queen ... Then great storm and you die." She was the woman whose death the emperor most mourned and he remembered her with tenderness all through his stay on Saint Helena.

Au Quartier Général Vérone le frimaire
An de la République Une et Indivisible

*Bonaparte* Général en Chef de L'Armée
d'Italie

## A Joséphine

Je ne t'aime plus du tout ; au contraire je te déteste. Tu es une vilaine, bien gauche, bien bête, bien Cendrillon. Tu ne m'écris point du tout, tu n'aimes pas ton mari ; tu sais le plaisir que lui font tes lettres, et tu ne lui en écris pas six lignes jetées au hasard.

Que faites-vous donc toute la journée, Madame ? Quelle affaire si importante vous ôte le temps d'écrire à votre bien bon amant ? Quelle affection étouffe et met de côté l'amour, le tendre et constant amour que vous lui avez promis ? Quel peut être ce merveilleux, ce nouvel amant qui absorbe tous vos instants, tyrannise vos journées et vous empêche de vous occuper de votre mari ? Joséphine, prenez garde, une belle nuit, les portes enfoncées, et me voilà.

En vérité, je suis en peine, ma bonne amie, de n'avoir point de vos nouvelles ; écrivez-moi vite quatre pages, et de ces aimables choses qui remplissent mon cœur de sentiment et de plaisir.

J'espère qu'avant peu je te serrerai dans mes bras et te couvrirai d'un million de baisers brûlants comme sous l'Équateur.

Mille baisers partout.

# Letter from Napoleon to Joséphine, 23 November 1796

This letter dated 23 November 1796 is the most striking proof of the young husband's love for Joséphine. The first words, "I do not love you an atom, on the contrary I detest you...", underline the passion of the young general-in-chief, left bereft at a lack of communication from his beloved.

**Translation**

To Joséphine, At Milan.

Verona, November 23, 1796

I don't love you an atom; on the contrary, I detest you. You are a good for nothing, very ungraceful, very tactless, very tatterdemalion. You never write to me; you don't care for your husband; you know the pleasures your letters give him, and you barely write him half a dozen lines, thrown off anyhow.

How, then, do you spend the livelong day, madam? What business of such importance robs you of the time to write to your very kind lover? What inclination stifles and alienates love, the affectionate and unvarying love which you promised me? Who may this paragon be, this new lover who engrosses all your time, is master of your days, and prevents you from concerning yourself about your husband? Joséphine, be vigilant; one fine night the doors will be broken in, and I shall be before you.

Truly, my dear, I am uneasy at getting no news from you. Write me four pages immediately, and some of those charming remarks which fill my heart with the pleasure of imagination.

I hope that before long I shall clasp you in my arms, and cover you with a million kisses as burning as if under the equator.

Bonaparte.

contract enshrining the separation of their properties before Joséphine's lawyer, Maître Ragideau, who sought to put her on her guard against this penniless young soldier.

The quiet ceremony took place at ten o'clock in the evening in the mairie of the second arrondissement, which was located in the Hôtel de Mondragon in the rue d'Antin. At ten in the evening, because, to the amazement of the bride and the four witnesses who included Barras and Tallien, the bridegroom was late. On the marriage certificate, Napoleon added a few months to his age, while for her part, Joséphine had magically become five years younger. For the young groom it was a matter of reducing the age gap between him and his wife to avoid possible mockery.

This marriage caused anger and amazement in the Bonaparte clan, as they had not given their consent and saw Joséphine as no more than an adventuress. The couple moved into an attractive private house in the rue Chantereine which Joséphine rented from the voluptuous Julie Carreau, the former mistress of the great actor Talma. But this was only for a few hours, as the general had to leave to rejoin his army in Italy. Later, after his return from Italy, Napoleon was able to acquire this house, which he did on 31 March 1798.

Throughout the campaign, Napoleon continually corresponded with Joséphine, by turns passionate or disappointed, depending on the information he had received from Paris about her infidelity. However, some of his missives betray absolute devotion to this woman, whom he idolized:

"Verona, 1st Frimaire, year V.

My darling Joséphine, I am going to bed, with my heart full of your adorable image and distressed by spending so much time away from you; but I hope that I will be happier in a few days and that I will have the chance to give you proof of the ardent love you have inspired in me. You don't write to me any more; you no longer think of your good friend, cruel woman! Don't you know that without you, without your heart, without your love, there is neither happiness nor life for your husband. Dear God! How happy I would be if I could watch you at your toilette, a little shoulder, a little white breast, springy, nice and firm; above them, a little face, with a scarf tied Creole fashion, good enough to eat. You know I haven't forgotten the little visits; you know, the little black forest. I kiss it a thousand times and wait impatiently to be there. It's all due to you, life, happiness, pleasure are only what you make them. To live in a Joséphine is to live in Elysium. To kiss your mouth, your eyes, your shoulder, your bosom, everywhere, everywhere!"

**Left:** *Having bought the Malmaison estate in 1799 for 325,000 francs, Joséphine commissioned the architects Percier and Fontaine to refurbish it. They applied new decorative concepts that would prove influential.*

## Eugène de Beauharnais (1781–1824)

Through his marriage to Joséphine, Napoleon gained two step-children to whom he showed great affection. Eugène, who became a soldier, probably brought about Napoleon's meeting with Joséphine by approaching him to claim the sword of his father, Alexandre, Vicomte de Beauharnais. Courageous and loyal, he became the arch-chancellor of the Empire, Prince of Venice and Viceroy of Italy. He and his sister Hortense were adopted by Napoleon.

**Above:** *Eugène de Beauharnais was always very close to his mother and quickly established a good relationship with his stepfather, who would later give him numerous posts, as well the title of Viceroy of Italy. His loyalty and devotion in various military campaigns made him a pillar of support for Bonaparte, particularly in Austria and Russia.*

# The First Italian Campaign

Only two days after marrying Joséphine, Bonaparte left to rejoin his troops on 11 March 1796. On 2 March, he had been appointed commander in chief of the army in Italy to replace General Schérer. He knew this army well as he had been its temporary leader after Toulon, but his closeness to Robespierre's brother had cost him the command.

Time was pressing. In fact, the situation on the border was catastrophic. With no uniforms and poorly shod, the troops had been neglected for several weeks. After resuming the direction of operations and drawing on the experience of the other generals under his authority, particularly the seasoned campaigners Masséna and Augereau, Napoleon soon got the measure of the situation.

As previously at Toulon and Paris, his early decisions did not fail to surprise. First, in a famous address of 27 March he won the confidence of his men, urging them to grasp their future with courage and tenacity: "Soldiers, you are naked and ill-fed; the Government owes you much, but can give you nothing.

*Below: On 13 April Bonaparte led his troops to victory over the Sardinians at Millesimo, where he also received the flags captured at Menotte and Cosseria from Marmont.*

*Opposite above: The Battle of Arcole raged for three days, until a turning point occurred on 15 November. Bonaparte led the assault, after recapturing his men's standard with Augereau. Napoleon later wrote, "Never has a battlefield been as fiercely contested as that of Arcole."*

*Opposite below: Napoleon's reputation was based not only on his crushing victories, but also on the passion of his speeches to the soldiers in Italy. His strength and charisma had a profound influence on these men living on a knife edge. In this text dated 20 May 1796 Napoleon emphasizes the courage of his "brothers in arms" who had "overturned, dispersed and scattered everything that lay in their way. ... Milan is yours and the Republican banner is flying all over Lombardy."*

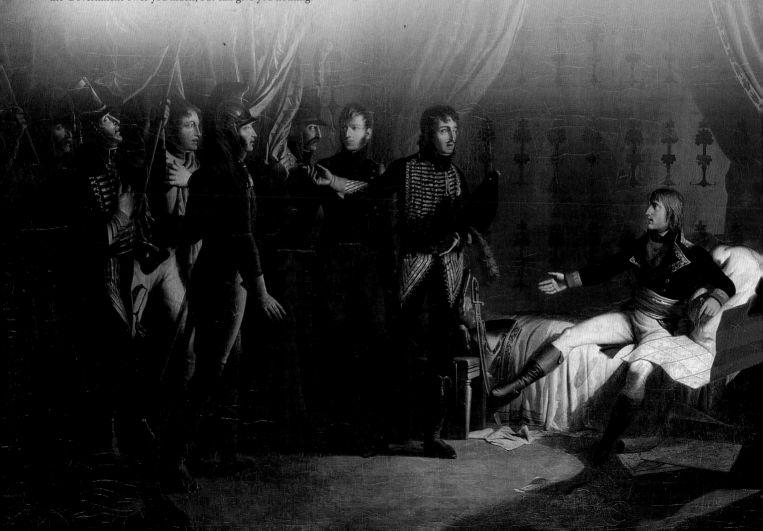

When Masséna and Napoleon first
met in 1796, the older Masséna did
not appear to give much credit to
this general-in-chief sent to him
from Paris. He probably imagined
Barras's man was just a cat's paw.
However, Napoleon's charm worked
on the former ship's boy, who
had enlisted in the Bataillon des
Volontaires du Var. At Rivoli in
1797, then two years later at Zurich,
Genoa, and finally at Essling and
Wagram in 1809, Masséna covered
himself with glory by alternating
attack and defence with unusual
intelligence. However, at the head
of the French armies in Portugal, his
failure to act in unity with the other
marshals who were with him in the
Peninsula marked the end of his
career under the Empire.

**Above:** *In his memoirs Napoleon was
unstinting in his praise of the man whom
he called, after Rivoli, "the beloved child of
Victory". Massena had "rare courage and
remarkable tenacity. When defeated, he was
always ready to start again as if he had been
the victor."*

Your patience, the courage you show in the midst of these rocky heights are admirable; but they will win you no glory, no splendour will reflect on you. I intend to lead you into the most fertile plains in the world. Rich provinces and great cities will be in your power; there you will find honour, glory and riches. Soldiers of Italy, will you lack courage or constancy?"

There was considerable enthusiasm. He turned these neglected men into powerful heroes. The first victories over the Austro-Sardinian troops confirm this feeling.

The general plan had been drawn up by Carnot, the Minister of War, and assigned a diversionary role to Bonaparte's troops, as all the major action was supposed to take place further north with Generals Jourdan and Moreau on the Rhine. But when the position appeared to be compromised, Bonaparte turned the situation to his advantage, making his mark as one of the great military strategists of his time. Blow by blow, he beat the Sardinians at Montenotte, Dego and then Millesimo.

Then it was the Austrians' turn to suffer defeat. Against their line of defence, which was intended to protect Lombardy and its capital Milan, he launched an enveloping manoeuvre and made himself the master of Lodi. He succeeded in getting his men to cross the Adda by a narrow wooden bridge. On 10 May 1796, the legend was written, as the general-in-chief himself later recounted:

"There were thirty cannons defending the Lodi bridge crossing. I placed all my artillery in a battery. The firing was very fierce for several hours. As soon as the army arrived, it formed a 'colonne serrée', with the 2nd battalion of carabiniers at the head, followed by all the battalions of grenadiers. ... This formidable column overthrew all opposition: the entire artillery was immediately removed ...; it sowed fear, flight and death on all sides; the enemy was scattered far and wide in the twinkling of an eye."

From then on Napoleon's destiny would play out on the national stage. Having gallicized his name at the start of this campaign, by losing forever the famous Corsican "u" of "Buonaparte", he realized that nothing now barred his way to supreme power. "After Lodi", he later said, "I no longer saw myself as a simple general but as a man called upon to influence the fate of a nation. I realized that I could become a crucial actor on our political stage. That was when the first spark of lofty ambition was born."

At Arcole, on 15 November 1796, while the French were pushed back to the other side of the river, their commander hastened to revive his men once more by recapturing the French standard that had just fallen into enemy hands. But while legend has always viewed this decisive moment as the start of the victory, it forgets the crucial role played by another general, Augereau. In fact, Bonaparte nearly died on this famous bridge, and owed his life to the sacrifice of his aide-de-camp Muiron, who positioned himself between Napoleon and the Austrians and fell under enemy fire. It was only the genius of the painter Gros and the many hastily ordered prints of his famous painting of *Napoleon on the Bridge at Arcole* that won him popular support and reinforced the legend.

A first truce allowed the troops to recover. But at Rivoli, on 14 January 1797, after witnessing the withdrawal of General Joubert de La Corona the previous day, Bonaparte successively beat the men commanded by Alvinczy, Quasdanovitch and Wukassovitch. Because of his commitment and the speed with which he executed the plan, it worked perfectly, largely thanks to the contribution of Masséna and the French 32nd demi-brigade. The defeat turned into a complete rout, with Murat in pursuit, and the fall of Mantua on 2 February.

After this final victory of the campaign which enabled Napoleon to dominate northern Italy, the gates of glory opened for Bonaparte. Like a plenipotentiary minister, he believed he was authorized to deal directly with the Austrian ambassadors and signed the Treaty of Campo Formio. The Congress of Rastadt set the final seal on his authority.

**Below:** *The French general-in-chief established what some considered to be a court on Isola Bella. Like a sovereign of old, but in the name of the French Republic, he organized theatre performances and reconstituted the forms of a new monarchy.*

## Pierre-Charles François Augereau (1757–1816)

When the future Duc de Castiglione enlisted at the age of seventeen in the regiment of the Bourgogne-Cavalerie, he was far from imagining how his career would turn out. After serving in the Prussian armies, then in Naples and Portugal, Augereau returned to France to serve as a sergeant in the Garde Nationale. The arrival of Napoleon saw him involved in an uninterrupted succession of victories: Montenotte, Millesimo, Lodi and especially Castiglione, where he distinguished himself. At Arcole, legend has forgotten his act of valour at the head of his troops. He served as Deputy to the Five Hundred, and was one of the first to be promoted to Marshal of the Empire, despite his opposition to the coup d'état of Brumaire. After Jena and Eylau, he served in Spain and then at Leipzig, and finally near Lyon in 1814.

**Above:** *The decisive battle of the Italian campaign took place in Rivoli. This confrontation would inevitably lead to a new distribution of roles.*

**Right:** *Augereau's outstanding service and, above all, his experience in battle made him a worthy servant of the Fatherland. This Parisian, the son of a domestic servant and a fruit seller, had overwhelmed Castiglione and, as Bonaparte's right-hand man, he was entrusted with the glorious mission of delivering the enemy standards to the Directory.*

de Hongrie et de Boheme, et la
République françoise, dans l'espace
de trente jours à dater d'aujourd'hui
ou plutôt si faire se peut, et les actes
de ratification en due forme seront
échangés à Rastadt.

Fait et signé à Campo Formio près
d'Udine le dix sept Octobre mil sept
cent quatre vingt dix sept, (: vingt-six
Vendémiaire, an six de la République
françoise, une et indivisible :)

Le Marquis de Gallo                    Bonaparte

Louis Comte Cobentzel

Le Comte de Merveldt
                    Geelhey

Le Baron de Degelmann

Le Directoire exécutif arrête et signe le présent traité de paix
avec sa Majesté l'Empereur et Roi de Hongrie et de Boheme, négocié
au nom de la République françoise par le Citoyen Bonaparte, Général
en Chef de l'Armée d'Italie, par le pouvoir du Directoire exécutif et
chargé de ses instructions à cet effet.

Fait au Palais national du Directoire exécutif le vingt brumaire
an six de la République françoise une et indivisible.

François (de Neufchâteau)            Merlin

            Barras            La Révellière-Lépeaux

## The Treaty of Campo Formio, 1797

By signing the Treaty of Campo Formio (now preserved in the National Archives in Paris), Bonaparte showed that he could now deal with the enemy directly.

**Translation**

...of Hungary and Bohemia, and of the French Republic, within a timescale of thirty days from today, or sooner if possible, and the acts of ratification duly enacted will be exchanged at Rastadt.

Written and signed at Campo Formio near Udine on seventeenth of October seventeen ninety-seven (: twenty-six Vendemiaire, sixth year of the French First Republic, one and indivisible).

Bonaparte

The Marquis of Gallo
Louis Count Cobenzl
The Count of Merveldt
Baron Degelmann

The Executive Directory issues and signs this present peace treaty with his Majesty the Emperor King of Hungary and of Bohemia, negotiated, in the name of the French Republic, by the citizen Bonaparte, general in chief of the army of Italy, authorised representative of the Executive Directory, and entrusted with its instructions in this matter.
Given at the national Palace of the Executive Directoire, on the fifth brumaire year six of the French Republic, one and indivisible.

François de Neufchateau

*(Other three signatures beneath are illegible)*

# The Egyptian Expedition

The next objective was to have been England, but studies carried out along the British coast did not augur success in the near future. It was clear the deficiencies of the French navy would make victory impossible to achieve. In fact, the Directory and its Foreign Minister, Talleyrand, were attempting to get rid of a general who was beginning to obstruct the ambitions of others. Still basking in the glory of his victories in Italy and influenced by his reading of the philosophers and the great travellers, Bonaparte wanted to appear as a "civilizing hero" through a new campaign. He was informed that he was to spread the "Enlightenment of Europe" in the East and to enable Egypt, with its rich and varied natural resources, to regain its past power. This was to be achieved with the aid of technological advances and through art.

In May 1798, on the quays of Toulon, crates of food and materials were loaded onto the ships preparing for departure. With more than 50,000 men – soldiers, technicians and 160 carefully chosen scientists, engineers and artists – and no less than 800 horses, Bonaparte set out on what is still seen as one history's legendary expeditions. On this occasion the navy was required to make a significant contribution, with almost 300 ships to transport men and materials, plus an escort of thirteen warships, six frigates and thirty-five smaller ships.

"Soldiers! You are about to undertake a conquest that will have an incalculable effect on world civilization and trade. You will inflict the most severe and most telling blow on England, before dealing her the death blow. A few days after we arrive, the Mameluke beys, who exclusively favour trade with England, snub our merchants and tyrannize the unfortunate inhabitants of the Nile, will cease to exist. The peoples among

whom we will be living are Mahommedans; their first article of faith is this: 'There is no God but God' and Mohammed is his prophet.' Do not contradict them; act with them as we acted with the Jews and the Italians; show respect for their muftis and their imams, as you did for the rabbis and the bishops. The Roman legions protected all religions. You will find customs here that are different from those in Europe: you will have to get used to them. The first city we will encounter was built by Alexander. At every step we take, we will find relics worthy of inspiring the French to emulate them."

The general-in-chief galvanized his troops with stirring words that would go down in posterity: "Soldiers, remember that forty centuries look down on you from the tops of these pyramids." The road to Cairo does indeed run past this unique site where the crucial attack was to be launched. But General Desaix, who was soon to conquer Upper Egypt and become known as "the Just Sultan" because of his kindness towards the local people, warned his men of the risks: "The commanders and officers are ordered not to allow the troops to get out of control or advance in skirmishing order unless the order is given. The corps must always stand and march in 'colonnes serrées'." That was the only solution when faced with an enemy that was mobile, courageous, but often disorganized – the Mamelukes, who were famous for their horsemanship.

*Below: The painter Lejeune depicted the confrontation between the French and the Mameluke horsemen, who were driven back into the Nile. Unconcerned about showing several of the day's events on a single canvas, Lejeune presented a modern tapestry of the exploits of the conquerors of the Orient.*

*Below right: Having encouraged the victor of Arcole and Rivoli to embark on a risky venture in the footsteps of the Pharaohs, Talleyrand, the former bishop of Autun, undoubtedly never dreamt that Bonaparte would come back shrouded in glory (despite the mixed success of the campaign), or that he himself would hold as important a post as that of the Minister of Foreign Affairs for almost a decade.*

## Charles-Maurice de Talleyrand-Périgord (1754–1838)

The altercation between Napoleon and the Minister for Foreign Affairs ("You are shit in a silk stocking") disparages rather than clarifies the delicate relationship that existed between the two men for almost twenty years. The former Bishop of Autun, who adapted to changing political regimes like no other before him, had a different idea of the permanence of power. Though he had long been Bonaparte's most heeded adviser, Talleyrand quickly became his enemy (it was he who sent the young general to Egypt) before he came to believe in the good fortune of this fiery, victorious Corsican. From Brumaire to Tilsit, their ambitions made an ideal combination (the decision to remove Duc d'Enghien is attributed to Talleyrand). After 1807, distrust regained the upper hand until the fall of Napoleon's Eagle. The "Limping Devil" (so-called because of a birth defect) came to an understanding with his worst enemy, the police chief Joseph Fouché, to offer the crown to Louis XVIII in 1814: power was always what mattered most.

The French army, consisting of five divisions, had been advancing for several days in square formation, in order to guard against all eventualities, and arrived on the banks of the Nile early on the morning of 21 July 1798. Under the gaze of the inhabitants of Cairo, who had hastened to the approaches to the battlefield, Mourad Bey unleashed his 6,000 horsemen in their colourful turbans, armour and golden helmets in a single charge at about three in the afternoon. The French, acting as one body, formed up in six rows of squares and repulsed the desperate attacks of the Mamelukes. Some of the attackers were forced to flee in boats towards Giza, the remainder (mostly horsemen) were drowned in the Nile.

After that, the road to Cairo lay open, despite the last resistance of men under the other Mameluke chief, Ibrahim Bey. On 1 August 1898, however, the Battle of the Nile in Aboukir Bay saw the French fleet sunk by the English under Nelson, making the French prisoners of those they had conquered. Their opponents predicted that "at the foot of these pyramids, built by their ancestors, the French will find their tombs and meet their fate!"

Nevertheless, Bonaparte now became the new Pharaoh of an ageless land, the heir of the Alexanders and Caesars, but also a modern head of state, bringing with him the teachings of the philosophers of the enlightenment. Himself a member of the French Institute, on 5 Fructidor, year VI (22 August 1798) Bonaparte founded an Egyptian Institute that initially had thirty-six members working across four sections: mathematics, physics, political economy, and literature and the arts. It was charged with three missions: to study the history of Egypt (artistic and natural), to bring the country out of its religious obscurantism and to modernize it, particularly from the point of view of irrigation.

Once the Cairo rebellion had been suppressed, Bonaparte intended to extend his influence to other territories. He created a dromedary regiment, which was much better adapted to the climatic conditions, and then launched his armies towards Upper Egypt with Desaix, while he led his troops towards Syria. The Battle of Mount Tabor saw eventual French victory against the Turks, and at Jaffa the dramatic conquest of the fort was followed by the massacre of its inhabitants. However, a long though ineffective siege of the British at Acre forced Napoleon to retreat.

On returning to Egypt, Bonaparte discovered a catastrophic situation had developed. The population was no longer willing to put up with the attitude of the French and had realized that power could well be exercised without them. The victory over the Mamelukes of Emir Mustapha Bey at Aboukir on 25 July 1799 helped them to forget the disastrous expedition that had turned into a fiasco. There were considerable losses: some 5,000 Turks were killed, wounded and taken prisoner, and 150 were killed and 750 wounded on the French side.

History also records that, not far from Rosetta, Lieutenant Pierre Bouchard discovered a granite stele carved with characters in three different types of writing: hieroglyphics, Greek and Demotic. A book known as the *Description de l'Égypte* was published, containing all the documentation gathered by the French scholars and offering a very detailed description of the archaeological discoveries, temples, populations, sculptures, as well as the flora and fauna

During the Egyptian expedition, Napoleon became infatuated with Pauline Fourès who had followed her husband, a soldier in the 22nd light infantry, dressed in army uniform. Better known as "Bellilote" (a nickname adapted from her maiden name), she was considered to be Napoleon's "official" mistress. However, she did not return to France and instead became the companion of Kléber, Bonaparte's successor in Cairo. Under the Consulate and the Empire, she was given a dowry and married again, this time to the Comte de Ranchoux.

encountered in the course of this epic expedition.

Having entrusted the command to General Kléber, Bonaparte returned to France. Between 30 September and 6 October 1799, after once again evading Nelson, who was cruising the Mediterranean, Napoleon called in at Ajaccio, accompanied by his faithful lieutenants, then landed at Fréjus.

**Far left:** *Bonaparte put down the Cairo Rebellion but later treated the local populace with magnanimity.*

**Above:** *After a long campaign and no real victory to show for it, Bonaparte accepted that his future lay in Paris and prepared to sail for France. First, however, he fought another battle in Aboukir, where his fleet had once been overwhelmed by the English. This time the French exacted their revenge in a bloody battle.*

**Left:** *The outstanding successes of the Egyptian expedition included several discoveries. The Rosetta stone, later deciphered by Champollion, enhanced our knowledge of hieroglyphics and, more generally, threw light upon an essential part of our heritage.*

**Above:** *Once Bonaparte found out about Joséphine's infidelities, he amused himself with the wife of one of his soldiers popularly known as Bellilote. This relationship was scandalous, but back in Paris Pauline Fourès would quickly be forgotten by Napoleon.*

# Brumaire

While the French troops in Egypt had partly succeeded in restoring their fortunes and improving their image, the disastrous news arriving from France – where a coup d'état in June 1799 had seen the moderates thrown out of the Directory and further disturbances in the continuing fray – had confirmed Bonaparte in the idea that he must return to France in order to put an end to the chaos and seize power. Newspapers he was given by the English during an exchange of prisoners lent support to his fears. The war with Austria had broken out again. Italy, which had been conquered so brilliantly two years earlier, was now in enemy hands. In Germany, the defeat at Stokach meant that the Austrians were once again on the banks of the Rhine. Only General Masséna, at Zurich on 25 and 26 September 1799, would manage to save what he could by defeating the Russian army under General Suvarov.

"Let us not wait for complete destruction: the malady would be incurable," said Bonaparte privately to his close friends. Having returned to Cairo on 11 August, he prepared his departure with the greatest secrecy. He surrounded himself with a few officers whom he knew to be absolutely loyal to him, such as Berthier, Marmont, Lannes, Murat, Duroc and Andréossy. "They were indispensable," he later said. "I had my project. I had to keep them with me." He is even said to have declared to General Menou, whom he left in Egypt, "I will reach Paris, I will drive out this flock of lawyers who care nothing for us and are incapable of governing the Republic, I will put myself at the head of the government …". Only Kléber, whose opposition Bonaparte had reason to fear, was not in on the secret. A simple, hastily scrawled letter informed him of Napoleon's departure and that he had been appointed to succeed him as commander of the army. The hot-headed Alsatian did not conceal his indignation at these actions, which he compared to dereliction of duty: "Our man [Napoleon] went off like a sub-lieutenant burning his palliasse after filling the cafés of the garrison with the scandal of his escapades …"

At dawn on 23 August 1799 Bonaparte left Egypt. His naval division, commanded by Rear-Admiral Ganteaume, consisted of only two frigates, the *Muiron*, which bore the name of the aide-de-camp who had saved his life at Arcole, and the *Carrère*, plus two light vessels, the *Revanche* and the *Fortune*. Worried by the sight of an English brig cruising off Alexandria, Ganteaume brought forward the departure. At this time of year there are usually winds blowing from the north-west. But by a miracle a

**Right:** *Returning as a hero from his expedition to Egypt and Syria, Bonaparte saw himself benefitting from the lamentable situation of the Directorial regime and seizing power unchallenged. He was not reckoning, however, on the power of the chambers, some of which were opposed to a new coup d'état.*

## Jean-Baptiste Kléber (1753–1800)

From Strasbourg, Kléber began his career in the 1st regiment of Hussars, but then studied architecture. However, after serving in the Army of the Rhine during the early years of the Revolution and participating in the victory of Fleurus under the orders of General Jourdan, he followed Bonaparte to Egypt. His victory at Mount Tabor enabled the army to return victorious from the difficult Syrian campaign. It was Kléber to whom Napoleon entrusted command of the troops when he left in 1799. But the following year, after a final victorious battle at Heliopolis, Kléber was assassinated in Cairo. This was on the very day when Napoleon, now First Consul, defeated the Austrians at Marengo.

**Above:** *Kléber, one of Bonaparte's most faithful lieutenants, was entrusted to safeguard French interests in Egypt, but the murder of this Alsatian general on 14 June 1800 spared him from witnessing the end of the oriental dream and the usurpation of power by the British.*

favourable breeze enabled the small flotilla to keep a sufficient distance from the English cruisers off Alexandria. On 13 September, the squadron was able to make good speed towards Sardinia. On 29 September, Bonaparte sighted the coast of Corsica, and two days later, on 1 October, the *Muiron* entered the harbour of Ajaccio. Napoleon spent a few days in the house where he was born. It was to be the last time; he would never return again. At dawn on 9 October, after 45 days at sea, the flotilla anchored off Saint-Raphaël in the Gulf of Fréjus.

Under the naval and health regulations of the time, anyone arriving from eastern countries where plague was rife was obliged to submit to quarantine measures. Of course there was no question of Bonaparte doing this, given the circumstances of his return. The situation in France was one of disorder: corruption reigned, while trade and industry were in ruins. Moreover, the crowd's enthusiasm for the returning heroes was such that, braving the risks of possible contagion, they clustered around the general and his companions, and literally carried them off the ships to bring them ashore. By a fortunate coincidence, it was the same day that news of the victory at Aboukir reached France. Everywhere the crowd hailed Napoleon as a saviour. A week later, crowned in glory, Bonaparte arrived triumphant in Paris. Bernadotte, who was trying to rekindle the Jacobin flame, suggested to Barras that he should have Napoleon arrested and tried as a deserter. "We are not equal to the task," sighed the Director and friend of Joséphine. Bonaparte had no further need to hesitate. The road to power lay open.

All Paris knew that Sieyès, author of the famous pamphlet *"Qu'est-ce que le tiers-état?"* ("What is the third estate?"), was looking for a "swordsman" to lead his coup d'état. Sieyès, who had made a study of constitutions, had lost Joubert at the Battle of Novi in August 1799. Then Moreau decided he could not live up to the political credit accorded to him. His monarchist sympathies were well known, and he refused to take on the responsibility. On hearing the news of Bonaparte's return, Moreau is said to have spoken to Sieyès in these words: "Look, this is our man! He will carry out your coup d'état much better than I could …"

On 18 Brumaire (9 November 1799), after several days of plotting and tough negotiations, Bonaparte was appointed commander of the Paris troops to protect the representatives of the nation from a hypothetical plot. The trap should have closed without a blow being struck. But they reckoned without the perspicacity of several of their opponents, fierce republicans and seasoned plotters.

The next day, the conspirators expected power to fall into their hands, but when General Bonaparte entered the provisional parliament in the Château de Saint-Cloud, he was greeted by jeering and cries of "outlaw!" from the deputies of the Council of Five Hundred.

**Left:** *After so much upheaval during its time at the head of the State, the Consulate sought political calm. A new era was opening up for Republican France at the start of the nineteenth century thanks to economic prosperity and peaceful relationships with its European neighbours.*

It took all the experience of Napoleon's younger brother Lucien, who had recently become the president of the Assembly, to prevent the confused speech made by the victor of Arcole and the Pyramids from turning into a farce. Napoleon, usually such a brilliant speaker when facing his troops, lost his composure and almost caused the plan that Sieyès had skilfully been preparing for several weeks to fail.

Legend has it that stilettos had been drawn by certain members of the parliament, in particular another Corsican by the name of Arena, in order to make an attempt on the life of the conqueror of Italy and Egypt. In their eyes he had become a potential dictator: "Get out, General. You don't know what you are saying!" But after recovering himself outside, Bonaparte addressed his soldiers, saying, "Troublemakers are talking about re-establishing their bloodthirsty domination, I wanted to speak to them, they answered me with daggers." In fact, the existence of the plot has never been confirmed.

It was Lucien who saved the situation with a brilliant theatrical gesture. He grasped his sword and held it against Napoleon's chest, declaring before 6,000 dumbfounded grenadiers, "I swear that I will pierce his heart if he ever renounces his love of the Republic." The calm of Lefebvre, combined with the passion of Murat, won the day. They contented themselves with reiterating the cry uttered by the victor of Aboukir when he entered the city: "Throw all those people out!"

Finally, on the evening of 10 November 1799, they managed to find enough deputies in favour of the plot to get the basis of the provisional Consulate adopted. A provisional triumvirate was appointed, consisting of Bonaparte, Sieyès and Roger-Ducos. Napoleon Bonaparte, aged just thirty, was now head of state.

Below: *Were it not for the decisive intervention of Lucien on 19 Brumaire, the coup would undoubtedly have failed. This atmospheric painting by Sablet uses chiaroscuro to present the debates in the Chamber of the Five Hundred, serving to heighten the drama of the situation still further.*

Below: *The First Consul would from now on be depicted in his characteristic uniform. In this painting by Jean-Baptiste Isabey, the legendary two-horned hat and hand-in-the-waistcoat are already in evidence.*

Below right: *The Abbé Sieyès was one of the main instigators of the numerous constitutions drawn up over the course of the revolutionary episode.*

## Emmanuel-Joseph Sieyès (1748–1836)

Better known for his famous pamphlet of January 1789 on the third estate, it was the regicide Sieyès who was largely responsible for Bonaparte's rise to power. Although he was one of the main theorists behind the republican constitutions, this former clergyman was overshadowed for a long time by the great thinkers of the Revolution, particularly Robespierre, who considered him too intellectual. He was elected to the Five Hundred after Thermidor and even became ambassador to Berlin. Having called on Bonaparte to carry out his coup d'état, after the events of Brumaire he was appointed as the first of the three provisional consuls. However, as Napoleon refused to take on the role of "puppet" intended for him, Sieyès was dismissed and became a senator for the Domaine de Crosne. President of the Senate, Count of the Empire, member of the Institute, he continued to accumulate honours until the time of the Hundred Days, when he entered the Chamber of Peers on 2 June 1815. Under the Restoration he was exiled as a regicide, only returning in 1830.

# Peace in Europe and the World

At the beginning of 1800, Napoleon had been First Consul for two months. In order to establish his power, he not only had to reorganize France which had been battered by ten years of revolution, but also to face the allies of the Second Coalition. Russia ceased to be a member of the coalition after Masséna's victory at Zurich in 1799, and after the Convention of Alkmaar Britain no longer had troops operating on the continent. Only Austria remained to be defeated. However, aware of the weakened state in which France had been left by the Directory, the Austrians decided to fight on alone and proposed to invade France.

Bonaparte now had three main armies at his disposal. The first, under Moreau on the Rhine, numbered 100,000 men. The second, with 40,000 men, was commanded by Masséna in the Genoa region, and the third, known as the reserve, was 50,000 men strong and stationed at Dijon. As for the Austrians, they had two main armies: 100,000 men in Germany headed by General Kray and 120,000 men in Italy under General Melas.

The French plan adopted was as follows: towards the end of April, Moreau would go on the offensive to push the enemy back into Bavaria and do everything possible to contain a counter-offensive, in order to give Bonaparte time to gather the reserve army and lead them across the Alps to unite with Masséna's army in Italy. Then, when all the forces had joined up, the First Consul would endeavour to destroy the Austrian army in Italy.

**Opposite below:** *Proud and unruffled astride a spirited horse, the new Caesar followed in the footsteps of Charlemagne and Hannibal by crossing the Alps. The painter David preserved for posterity not only the journey through the Great Saint-Bernard Pass but also history in the making.*

**Below:** *In this detailed rendering of the Battle of Marengo, Lejeune proved both a war reporter and a propagandist. The decisive moment when General Desaix and his forces came to the rescue of Bonaparte and Berthier, gave the advantage to the French.*

## Louis Charles Antoine des Aix (1768–1800)

After first enlisting in the royal armies against the advice of his family, this young Auvergne nobleman known as Desaix joined the Republican troops. Appointed brigadier-general in October 1793, he was head of the Army of the Rhine until he met Bonaparte. In Egypt, after the Battle of the Pyramids he had to go back up the Nile Valley in pursuit of Mourad Bey, whom he succeeded in defeating. He was appointed governor of Upper Egypt and behaved with great humanity towards the Egyptians, who soon gave him the nickname "the Just Sultan". It was he who signed the Convention of El Arich on 24 January 1800 with the English and the Turks on the evacuation of Egypt – but this did not prevent him from being taken prisoner. When he was freed, he rejoined the army in Italy, but despite his crucial intervention, he lost his life at Marengo on 14 June 1800.

**Above:** *In this splendid portrait by the Italian artist Appiani, the young General Desaix, known to the Egyptians as "the just Sultan", is idealized as a martyr for freedom.*

Following the example of Hannibal and Charlemagne, Napoleon chose the Great Saint-Bernard Pass route across the Alps to gain time on the enemy. But the crossing took place in extreme conditions, as Coignet reports in his *Mémoires*. Although David later painted a striking picture of the young general sitting calmly on a spirited horse, in reality the army crossed the Alps on the backs of mules and the newly appointed consul almost lost his life during the journey. On the road along the Po valley, their progress was slowed by the capture of the fort of Bard and this prevented some of the cannon from getting through. When they arrived in Milan on 2 June, the French were acclaimed by the inhabitants. However, Masséna's surrender in Genoa meant that the troops were unable to savour their moment of glory. The Austrian troops were on their way and intent on waging a decisive battle against the French. It took place at Marengo on 14 June 1800.

Against all expectations, the day began disastrously for the French. Having dispersed his troops too early because he did not believe that he was yet facing all the enemy troops, Bonaparte was caught by General Ott's flank attacks. On the French side, first Lannes and then Victor were forced to retreat through lack of ammunition. At two in the afternoon, while replenishing his army's supplies, Bonaparte withdrew his lines to San Giuliano. A simple Austrian cavalry attack should have decided the outcome of the battle and the Austrian commander, Melas, already sensing victory, left to announce this resounding French defeat to the Austrian emperor.

At five o'clock, everything changed when 8,000 Hungarian grenadiers arrived in a column attempting to overthrow all that was in their path. At that moment General Desaix arrived at the head of General Boudet's division and, according to legend, announced: "A battle has been lost, but it is only five o'clock, and there is time to win another one." As one man, "the army rallied, returned to the charge, encountered the enemy, and General

Desaix was killed by the first shot of the engagement." This action enabled the right wing with Victor, Lannes, Monnier and above all the Guards to regroup. Kellermann's leading role in the French cavalry charges was absolutely crucial. The French won a total victory and thus the First Consul inaugurated his reign with a brilliant coup.

After so many years of internecine fighting, what the country really needed was civil calm. The peace treaty with Austria signed at Lunéville on 9 February 1801 and even more the Treaty of Amiens with Britain signed on 25 March 1802 had huge repercussions. As the newspapers and writings of the time reported, "by this peace, the Revolution was consolidated, equality conquered, the possession of national property guaranteed, the dream of all in France, [who worked] on the land, in workshops, and in shops; the dream of the bourgeois and the peasants – and also the dream of many soldiers" was realized. For a very long time, "the workers continued to talk about the peace and the First Consul with almost indescribable enthusiasm. Their confidence in the government was boundless"; and "Bonaparte appeared as the man of peace."

**Below:** *After eight years of relentless conflict between France and the allied monarchies, peace became a reality. Festivities were organized all over Europe amidst unbridled enthusiasm.*

**Left:** *The allegorical figure of Peace here assumes the image of the First Consul, a veritable incarnation of glory and prosperity. Prudhon's work was presented in the Salon to great acclaim.*

# The Consular Reforms

A few days after Bonaparte, Sieyès and Roger-Ducos took office, Napoleon used his influence as First Consul to have the other two men replaced by Lebrun and Cambacérès. The new consuls were said to be "close" to his political ideas. Talleyrand had advised Napoleon that a man who is gradually imposing himself as the true head of state should be able to concentrate all power in himself: "The First Consul must have control of all matters directly relating to policy, that is to say the Ministry of the Interior and the Police for internal affairs, my own ministry [Foreign Affairs] for external affairs, and then the two major means of conducting warfare – the Ministries of War and the Navy."

From December 1799, Napoleon's first reforms began to bear fruit. Among the new institutions created was the Council of State, which was installed in the Petit-Luxembourg, the seat of government. There were a number of assassination attempts aimed at destabilizing this consular policy, particularly one that took place at Christmas 1800 in the rue Saint-Nicaise, while Napoleon was on his way to the opera with Joséphine to hear Haydn's *Creation*. In the end, the failure of the attempt acted as a catalyst and resulted in Bonaparte achieving absolute power. He was granted the freedom to "present his successor to the Senate, a significant step towards the right of inheritance", before being accorded the title of "First Consul for Life", with no sign of resistance from a conservative Tribunat and Senate who feared a restoration of the Bourbon

monarchy. The wish of the representatives of the people was confirmed by a plebiscite.

During the time of the Consulate, Napoleon was determined to make profound changes to society. He wanted to restore frameworks and boundaries, what he called "the blocks of granite". Many important reforms would be launched and come into being throughout Napoleon's reign.

The first was the Concordat of 1801, which regulated the relationship between the State and the Catholic Church. The alliance with the Church was a political response to a social necessity, making it possible to "dissociate the cause of the monarchy from that of a religion to which the French generally remained attached". Agreement had to be reached "in order to regulate the moral and social order, through its ministers and its teaching; to take on the tasks of education and assistance for which the state cannot take responsibilty." On 18 Germinal, year X (8 April 1802), the legislative body of the French Republic adopted and promulgated the text signed on 15 July of the previous year with Pius VII.

**Opposite:** *The Council of State, one of the main institutions established by the Consulate, was installed in the Petit-Luxembourg during the early days of the regime. The ceremony was attended by Secretary Locré and the presidents of the various sections, Brune, Ganteaume, Boulay de la Meurthe, Roederer and Defermon.*

**Below right:** *As Duke of Parma under the Empire, Jean-Jacques-Régis de Cambacérès was one of the leading figures in the Consular and Imperial regimes, with a decisive influence on ministerial decisions.*

**Below:** *Although Napoleon shared power with Cambacérès and Lebrun, in effect he imposed himself as supreme ruler within an organization which gradually turned into a hereditary regime.*

# Jean-Jacques-Régis de Cambacérès (1753–1824)

Originally from Montpellier, Cambacérès was one of the most important jurists of the end of the Ancien Régime. After making himself indispensable to the Convention and then to the Directory with his advice and innovations, he became Bonaparte's principal civilian collaborator. Like Berthier in military matters, Cambacérès may be seen as the alter ego of the head of state. As Second Consul and later Arch-Chancellor, he advised and even deputized for Napoleon when he was away on campaign. Most notably, it was Cambacérès who officially proclaimed him Emperor of France at Saint-Cloud on 18 May 1804. Together with the lawyer Portalis he provided the inspiration for the Civil Code. He guaranteed institutions and even ensured the smooth running of the government at the most critical times for the Empire when presiding over the Regency Council.

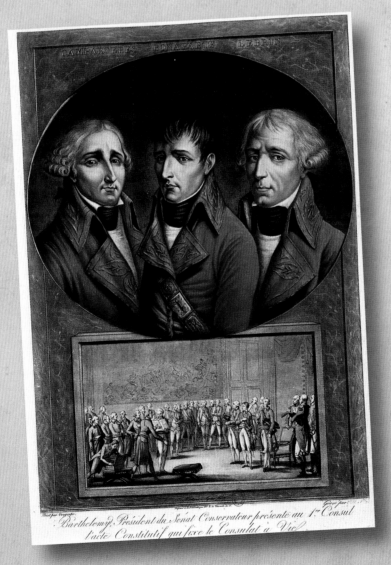

CAMBACÉRÈS BONAPARTE LEBRUN

*Barthelemy, Président du Sénat Conservateur présente au 1er Consul l'acte Constitutif qui fixe le Consulat à Vie.*

After religion Napoleon turned his attention to society. The Civil Code, known as the Code Napoléon after 1807, was promulgated on 21 March 1804. This laid down the rules of social behaviour and the Code of Civil Procedure. It was followed by the Commercial Code on 20 September 1807, the Code of Criminal Procedure on 27 November 1808, and the Penal Code on 22 February 1810.

Reforms to the education system were also made. The law of 1 May 1802 (11 Floréal, year X) established the lycées while the baccalaureate examination was introduced in 1808. The Imperial University came into being through the decree of 17 March 1808.

In 1802 Napoleon also launched a plan for a new honour. Strictly speaking, it would neither be an order of chivalry or a decoration. The plan was presented to the legislature on 15 May and adopted four days later. However, in the eyes of many people, it called equality into question, re-establishing a class of nobility with titles and revenues. In fact, Bonaparte's aim was to create a new elite based solely on merit. The Legion of Honour would be awarded to both soldiers and civilians who had helped to establish or defend the principles of the Revolution.

The first awards were made on 24 September 1803, and the first presentation of the crosses to civilians took place in the Church of Saint Louis des Invalides on 15 July 1804. The soldiers received their awards at the Camp de Boulogne on 16 August the same year. That morning, a grand spectacle was staged at the Camp de Boulogne. The entire army surrounded a hill, on which the throne of Dagobert was placed. Napoleon had the new members of the Legion swear an oath. With the same fervent enthusiasm, they all shouted "I swear". Then those fortunate enough to have been honoured came up in turn to receive the first cross with its beautiful red ribbon from the hand of the emperor. Deeply moved, some of them wept with joy, because they knew that this red ribbon represented the blood shed for France.

**Right:** *The Concordat of 1801 ended the schism created by the Revolution between the French State and the papacy, and restored, in theory, the Vatican's civil status in France. However, Napoleon made the Organic Articles a condition of the agreement which enabled the State to maintain control over Catholics (and Protestants) in France, thus upsetting the Vatican further. The articles also offered freedom to all religions for the first time.*

**Centre:** *The Legion of Honour was awarded for the first time in a solemn ceremony on 15 July 1804 in the Church of the Invalides, the day after the fifteenth anniversary of the storming of the Bastille. The new emperor, seated on a throne, personally bestowed the cross with a red ribbon on various distinguished figures.*

**Opposite below right:** *Joseph Fouché, the Minister of Police and a former regicide, ruthlessly controlled the country's apparati of information, censorship and espionage, using all his powers to achieve his ends.*

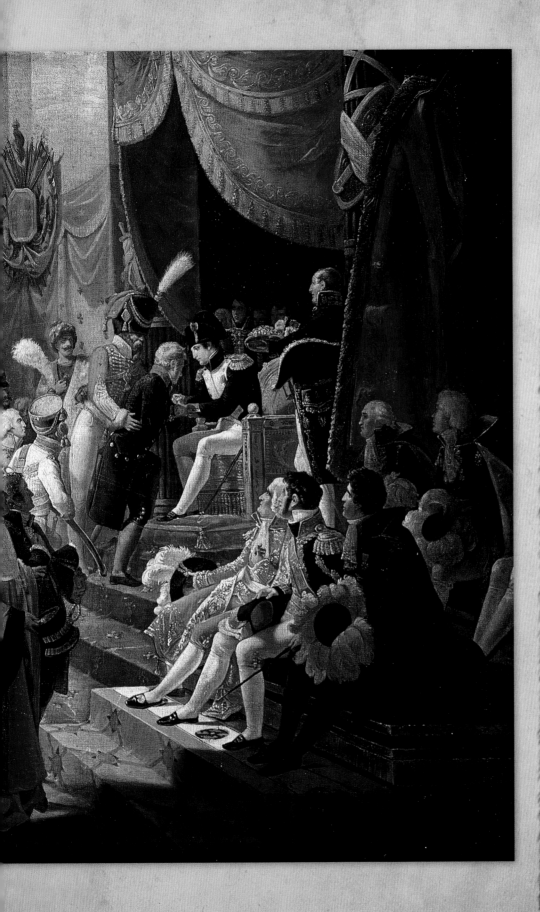

## Joseph Fouché
## (1759–1820)

A Jacobin, regicide, and organizer of the bloody massacres in Lyon where he was sent to quash a rebellion against the Convention, Fouché became one of the most influential figures under the Directory and especially under the Consulate through his central position as Minister of Police. A powerful and educated man, he was removed by Bonaparte for a time, despite the efficiency with which he pursued those responsible for the assassination attempt in the rue Saint-Nicaise. However, he returned to his post after foiling the most dangerous plots, notably that organized by the Chouan Cadoudal. After the death of the Duc d'Enghien, Fouché proposed the rank of emperor in order to put an end to any possibility of the Bourbon monarchy returning to France. However, he was dismissed again in 1810, in favour of Savary, and showed his opposition until the end of Napoleon's reign. In 1815, he persuaded the Senate to vote for the downfall of the emperor in favour of what he had long fought against – the arrival of Louis XVIII to the throne.

# Minute de Décret Impérial.

## Sommaire du Décret.

Au Palais de Erfurt — le 12 octobre 1808

### Napoléon, Empereur des Français, Roi d'Italie et Protecteur de la Confédération du Rhin,

art 1er.

nous avons anciens et accordons l'aigle et la légion —
d'Honneur aux sieurs.

Goethe, conseiller intime de Mr de Weimar
Wieland id
Starcke médecin major d'Iéna
Vogel Bourguemestre de d'Iéna
art 2

notre Grand Chancelier de la légion d'Honneur est
Chargé de l'exécution du présent décret.

Nap.

# Decree awarding the Légion d'Honneur

Minutes of the decree signed by Napoleon in Erfurt on 12 October 1808; it bestowed the eagle of the Légion d'Honneur on Goethe, Wieland, Starke and Vogel.

**Translation**

Minute of Imperial Decree.
Summary of the Decree.

Palace of Erfurt 12th October 1808
Sent on 20th October
to the Ministries of War and Finance
Napoleon, Emperor of the French People,
King of Italy and Protector of the
Rhine Confederation,
We thereby grant the Eagle of the Légion d'Honneur to the undersigned:

Goethe    personal adviser to the Duke of Weimar
Wieland   inf[antry?]
Strarke   Medical Officer of Iena
Vogel     Burgermaster of Iena
          (one word underneath illegible)

Our Grand Chamberlain of the Légion d'Honneur is tasked with carrying out this decree.

Napoleon

Classification des
Loix du Cod. Civil

Orateurs
Lesf. Portalis, rapporteur
Bigot-préameneu
Treilhard.

# Conseil d'État.

## Extrait du Registre des Délibérations.

Séance du Vingt Sept Ventôse an douze de la République.

## Projet de Loi

Concernant la réunion des loix civiles en un Seul Corps
de loix, Sous le titre de Code Civil des français

### Art. 1er

Seront réunies en un Seul Corps de loix, Sous le
titre de Code Civil des français, les lois qui Suivent, Savoir:

Présentation le 24 Ventôse
Discussion le 30 —

Approuvé
Le Second Consul

1°. Loi du 14 ventôse an 11. Sur la Publication, les effets et
l'application des lois en général.

2°. Loi du 17 Ventôse an 11. Sur la jouissance et la privation
des Droits Civils.

3°. Loi du 20 ventôse an 11. Sur les actes de l'État Civil.

4°. Loi du 23 ventôse an 11. Sur le domicile.

5°. Loi du 24 ventôse an 11. Sur les absens.

6°. Loi du 26 ventôse an 11. Sur le mariage.

7°. Loi du 30 ventôse an 11. Sur le Divorce.

8°. Loi du 2 Germinal an 11. Sur la paternité et la filiation.

9°. Loi du 2 Germinal an 11. Sur l'adoption et la Tutelle
officieuse.

10°. Loi du 3 Germinal an 11. Sur la puissance paternelle.

11°. Loi du 5 Germinal an 11. Sur la minorité, la Tutelle et
l'émancipation.

12°.

# The Civil Code Bill, 1804

Of all the codes published by the Consulate and then the Empire, the Civil Code was undoubtedly the most important as regards the organization of society. It was promulgated in March 1804 and named the Napoleonic Code under the Second Empire; even today, it still stands as one of the fundaments of contemporary France, and also of numerous other countries that adopted it or were directly influenced by it.

# Long Live the Emperor

Immediately after being proclaimed emperor on 18 May 1804 (28 Floréal, year XII), Napoleon made contact with the pope through the Papal Legate, Cardinal Caprara. Imagining himself as the heir of Charlemagne, he wanted the Sovereign Pontiff to come and preside at the inauguration ceremony of his regime which was to take place on 2 December. After prolonged negotiations (mainly diplomatic), Pius VII arrived in Paris after a stop at Fontainebleau.

The pope stayed in the Pavillon de Flore, leaving for Notre-Dame at nine o'clock in the morning. Following a centuries-old tradition, Pius VII was preceded by his Apostolic Nuncio bearing a silver-gilt cross and mounted on his famous mule. After being greeted by Cardinal de Belloy at the foot of the

great staircase of the archbishop's palace, he then entered the grand salon which had been reserved for him to put on his vestments. While Napoleon, Joséphine and the only two French princes present, Joseph and Louis Bonaparte, were received in turn by the Archbishop of Paris, the emperor is said to have whispered to his elder brother, "Joseph, if only our father could see us now!"

Then, in the choir of the cathedral, the pope had the emperor take an oath that he would henceforth "enforce respect the law, dispense justice …, maintain peace in the Church of God …, and ensure that the Pontiffs of the Church enjoy the respect and honour due to them in accordance with the holy canons". Then Napoleon advanced with Joséphine to the foot of the

**Below:** *On 18 May 1804 Cambacérès and several representatives of the Conservative Senate came to Saint-Cloud to read Napoleon Bonaparte the proclamation that made him emperor of the French. In the presence of Joséphine and members of his family, the ceremony sealed the creation of a Fourth Dynasty.*

**Right:** *Placing himself in direct line with his Carolingian predecessors, Napoleon surrounded himself with symbols of power that recalled or had belonged to the reign of Charlemagne. The crown was the main exhibit in a selection of regalia.*

**Below right:** *Pope Pius VII was invited to Paris for Napoleon's coronation and received an enthusiastic welcome from the crowd. His stay in Paris became a religious plebiscite, despite the adjustments made by the imperial administration in the ceremony performed in Notre-Dame on 2 December.*

## Pius VII (1742–1823)

Pius VII's captivity in Fontainebleau in 1812 – he had aligned with the allies against Napoleon after the emperor appended articles to the Concordat thereby giving the State control over the Church – and the famous saying (probably apocryphal) "commediante, tragediante" (comedian, tragedian) have made Pius VII a symbol of the opposition to the power of the emperor. However, we must not forget that his election in 1799 was greatly influenced by Bonaparte's French countrymen in Italy, that he agreed to the successive Concordats (French, Italian and German), and attended Napoleon's coronation in order to regain his own temporal power over the Transalpine States and the Papal Legations. He also refused to recognize Jerome's divorce and Joseph's sovereignty over the Kingdom of the Two Sicilies. Despite everything, he was very attached to the Bonaparte family, and after the restoration of the monarchy, he offered Napoleon's mother and her children a home and his protection.

high altar to be thrice anointed "once on the head, then once on each hand" by Pius VII in person. This had only been made possible by the religious marriage of the imperial couple the day before, as the empress had informed the pope that no religious ceremony had taken place since their civil wedding in 1796.

For the actual coronation, after the holy oil had been wiped away from their foreheads, Pius VII blessed the "imperial ornaments" (sword, cloaks, rings and orb). Then, after giving "la main de justice" (the symbol of the hand of justice) to Arch-Chancellor Cambacérès and the sceptre to Arch-Treasurer Lebrun, Napoleon crowned himself in front of the dumbfounded spectators. Only the pope had been made aware of this change to the ritual. Finally, Napoleon seized the second crown and held it above his head for an instant before going over to the kneeling Joséphine and gently placed it on her head. This is the moment immortalized by David in the painting, now in the Louvre; Napoleon's mother was painted in by the artist at the last moment: she did not in fact attend the coronation, having preferred to go to Rome with Napoleon's brothers Lucien and Jerome who had quarrelled with him for not having followed their mother's matrimonial "advice".

The imperial couple then walked in procession to the great throne. After the offertory and communion, the pope pronounced the Vivat and Napoleon took the constitutional oath from the great throne. He swore to "maintain the integrity of the territory of the Republic, to respect and enforce respect for the laws of the Concordat and freedom of worship, to respect and enforce respect for equality of rights, political and civil liberty, the irrevocability of the sale of national possession, not to raise any levies or taxes except under the law, to maintain the institution of the Legion of Honour, to govern solely to further the interests, happiness and glory of the French people".

**Above:** *David originally depicted the emperor's self-coronation but eventually transformed Napoleon's gesture into the crowning of Joséphine. When the couple visited the artist's studio in January 1808, Napoleon exclaimed: "David, you have read my thoughts, you have made me a French knight!"*

**Right:** *At the end of the ceremony the emperor took the constitutional oath.*

Three days later on 5 December, a military ceremony for the presentation of the flags and eagles to the troops was held in Paris on the Champ de Mars in front of the École Militaire – in exactly the same place where the young Bonaparte had begun his career. As he solemnly made a speech, the morning storm ceased and the emperor proclaimed, "Soldiers, here are your flags; these eagles will always serve you as a rallying point; they will be everywhere your emperor considers necessary for the defence of his throne and his people. You swear to sacrifice your life to defend them and maintain them constantly with your courage on the road to victory. Do you swear?" England, Austria and Russia had been warned – a new campaign could begin at any time.

**Below:** *The military ceremony, planned for the day after the coronation but eventually taking place on 5 December 1804, was recorded for posterity by the painter David as a stirring declaration of the army's commitment to its leader. It was finished in 1810 around the time of Napoleon's marriage to Marie-Louise, and so Joséphine was ultimately painted out; the space she left vacant was occupied by the leg of her son Eugène.*

(S'il s'agit d'une loi) le corps législatif a rendu, le ....... (la date) le décret suivant, conformément à la proposition faite au nom de l'Empereur, chacun après avoir entendu les orateurs du conseil d'État et des Sections du Tribunat le .......

« Mandons et ordonnons que les présentes, revêtues des Sceaux de l'État, insérées au bulletin des loix, soient adressées aux cours, aux tribunaux et aux autorités administratives, pour qu'ils les inscrivent dans leurs registres, les observent et les fassent observer : et le grand-juge Ministre de la justice est chargé d'en surveiller la publication. »

### Art: 141.

Les expéditions exécutoires des jugements sont rédigées ainsi qu'il suit:

N. (le prénom de l'Empereur), par la grâce de Dieu et les constitutions de la République, — Empereur des français, à tous présens et avenir, Salut.

La cour de ....... ou le tribunal de ....... (si c'est un tribunal de 1re instance), a rendu le jugement suivant.

(Ici copier l'arrêt ou le jugement.)

« Mandons et ordonnons à tous huissiers sur ce requis, de mettre ledit jugement à exécution; à nos procureurs généraux, et à nos procureurs près les tribunaux de 1re instance, d'y tenir la main; à tous commandans et officiers de la force publique, de prêter main-forte lorsqu'ils en seront légalement requis.

En foi de quoi le présent jugement a été signé par le président de la cour ou du tribunal et par le greffier.

### Titre XVI et Dernier.

### Art: 142.

La proposition suivante sera présentée à l'acceptation du peuple dans les formes déterminées par l'arrêté du 20 Floréal an X.

« Le peuple veut l'hérédité de la dignité impériale dans la descendance directe, naturelle, légitime et adoptive de Napoléon Bonaparte, et dans la descendance directe, naturelle et légitime de Joseph Bonaparte et de Louis Bonaparte, ainsi qu'il est réglé par le Sénatus-consulte organique de ce jour. »

Signé Cambacérès, Second Consul, Président; Morard-de-Galles, Joseph Cornudet, Secrétaires.

Vu et Scellé le Chancelier du Sénat, Signé Laplace.

Mandons et ordonnons que les présentes, revêtues des Sceaux de l'État, insérées au bulletin des loix soient adressées aux cours, aux tribunaux, et aux autorités administratives, pour qu'ils les inscrivent dans leurs registres, les observent et les fassent observer : et le grand juge Ministre de la justice est chargé d'en surveiller la publication.

Donné au Palais de St Cloud, le 28 Floréal an XII.

Napoléon

Vu par nous archi-chancelier de l'Empire.

Cambacérès

Par l'Empereur.

Le Secrétaire d'État.

Hugues B. Maret

Le Grand Juge - Ministre de la Justice.

Régnier

# Decree of Empire, 18 May 1804

The Empire was established in France by this organic sénatus-consulte dated 28 Floréal of year XII (18 May 1804). Its 142 articles detailed the new rules governing the powers entrusted to the Emperor of the French under the name of Napoleon I.

**Translation**

[Document continues…]
(And as it concerns a law) the legislative body enacted, on …… (the date) the following decree, in accordance with the proposal made in the name of the Emperor, and after having heard the speakers in the Council of State and the sections of the tribunal on …..

We Mandate and Order that the present document, bearing the seals of State, be inserted into the bulletin of laws and be addressed to the courts, tribunals and administrative authorities, so that they may inscribe them in their registers, observe them and ensure that they are observed; and the senior judge, Minister of Justice is responsible for supervising the publication thereof."

### Art: 141.

The execution of judgements shall be drawn up as follows:

N. (first name of the Emperor), by the grace of God and the constitutions of the Republic.

Emperor of the French to all present and future, Greetings.

The court of ….. or the tribunal of … (if it is a court of the first instance [a lower court]), has rendered the following judgement:

(copy the order or judgement here)

We Mandate and Order all bailiffs appointed for the purpose, to issue the said judgement for execution; it is for our state prosecutors and our prosecutors attached to the courts of the first instance to lend them assistance; and all commanders and officers of the forces of law and order are to assist them if they are required to do so in law.

By virtue of which the present judgement has been signed by the presiding judge of the court or tribunal, and by the clerk of the court

### Title XVI and Last
### Art: 142

The following proposal shall be submitted for acceptance by the people, in the forms determined by the decree of 20 Floreal, year X:

The people wish for the succession of the imperial dignity to pass down in the direct, natural, legitimate and adoptive descendant line of Napoleon Bonaparte, and in the direct, natural, legitimate and adoptive descendant line of Joseph Bonaparte and of Louis Bonaparte, as has been settled by the decision of the Senate this day.

Signed Cambacères, Second consul, President; Morard-de Galles, Joseph Cornudet, Secretary.

Seen and sealed by the Chancellor of the Senate, signed La Place.

We Mandate and Order that the present document, bearing the seals of State, be inserted into the bulletin of laws and be addressed to the courts, tribunals and administrative authorities, so that they may inscribe them in their registers, observe them and ensure that they are observed; and the senior judge, Minister of Justice is responsible for supervising the publication thereof.

Given at the Palace of St.-Cloud, on 28 Floréal, year XII.

[signature] Napoleon

Seen by us Arch-chancellor of the Empire
[signature]

By the Emperor:
The Secretary of State
[signature]

The Senior Judge, Minister of Justice.
[signature]

# The Austerlitz Campaign

Napoleon's continuing expansionist plans and the British reluctance to relinquish Malta saw Britain and France back on a war footing in May 1803. Determined once again to defeat his enemy and mount an invasion, Napoleon co-opted the Spanish, who declared war on Britain in December the following year. The decisive sea battle was fought in the Mediterranean at the Battle of Trafalgar on 21 October 1805, when Nelson annihilated the combined Franco-Spanish fleet. Though the victory gave the British command of the seas, its naval hero Nelson was killed in the battle, dying three hours after being struck by a musket ball.

In the meantime, the 30,000-strong French army had set off from the camps at Boulogne, where they had been preparing to invade Britain. But when attack by Villeneuve's fleet was delayed as it waited for reinforcements in the summer of 1805, Napoleon decided to send all his forces back to fight against Austria. A recently formed coalition between Britain, Austria, Russia, Sweden and Naples had just attacked Napoleon's new ally Bavaria. In less than three months, Napoleon unleashed his seven army corps led by his faithful lieutenants, mostly newly promoted marshals, towards the borders of Germany and Austria.

After a long siege of the city of Ulm and with no hope of support from his Russian allies, the Austrian General Mack surrendered on 20 October 1805, the day before the Battle of Trafalgar. Standing at the foot of the Michelsberg, Napoleon watched the surrendering enemy army of almost 30,000 men with their flags and more than sixty cannons file past. "He was standing on a high embankment, with his infantry behind him, drawn up in a semicircle on the slopes of the hills and opposite them his cavalry deployed in a straight line. The Austrians marched between them, laying down their weapons at the entrance to this natural amphitheatre …" Napoleon could not hide his delight. "My soldiers are my children," he said. The capture of the city made a huge impression. Less then a month later, on 14 November 1805, Napoleon received the keys to Vienna. All that remained for him to do was to confront the last remnants of the forces of the Austro-Russian coalition.

Napoleon wanted to take advantage of the withdrawal of the Russian armies under Kutuzov so as to take an enemy with superior numbers of troops (approximately 85,000 versus 75,000) by surprise. This force was intending to join up with the reinforcements led by the Austrian archdukes John and Charles, who had been pursued all the way from Italy by Masséna and Bonaparte's step-son Eugène. Napoleon chose Austerlitz in the region of Brünn (present-day Brno) as the location for the final confrontation with the Austrian emperor Francis II and Tsar Alexander I of Russia.

Despite the absence of the second, sixth and seventh corps, Napoleon entrusted the right wing, between the villages of Telnitz and Sokolnitz, to Davout and gave Lannes and Murat command of the left wing to thwart the actions of the Russian cavalry. On the day before the battle, he had let it be known that his troops

Below: *The breaking of the Treaty of Amiens led France to redeploy its armies. In order to oversee the preparations for the invasion of England, Napoleon made frequent visits to Boulogne and the surrounding area.*

Above: *Once he had turned his strategic attention towards central Europe, Napoleon unleashed his military might and won many spectacular battles. After the Siege of Ulm, 30,000 Austrian soldiers led by General Mack marched past Napoleon and symbolically laid down their arms and handed over the keys to the city.*

## Horatio, Viscount Nelson, Duke of Bronté (1758–1805)

It is no exaggeration to say that, together with Wellington, Nelson was Napoleon's greatest enemy. Having gone to sea at the age of twelve, this clergyman's son became a vice-admiral just five years later. After losing an eye in Corsica and an arm at Tenerife, he crossed Bonaparte's path in Egypt, sinking his fleet at Aboukir Bay in August 1798. Seven years later, on 21 October 1805, he was victorious at the crucial Battle of Trafalgar but died during the fighting. He entered the pantheon of the greatest British admirals because of his incomparable bravery and tactical sense. His statue now dominates London's Trafalgar Square.

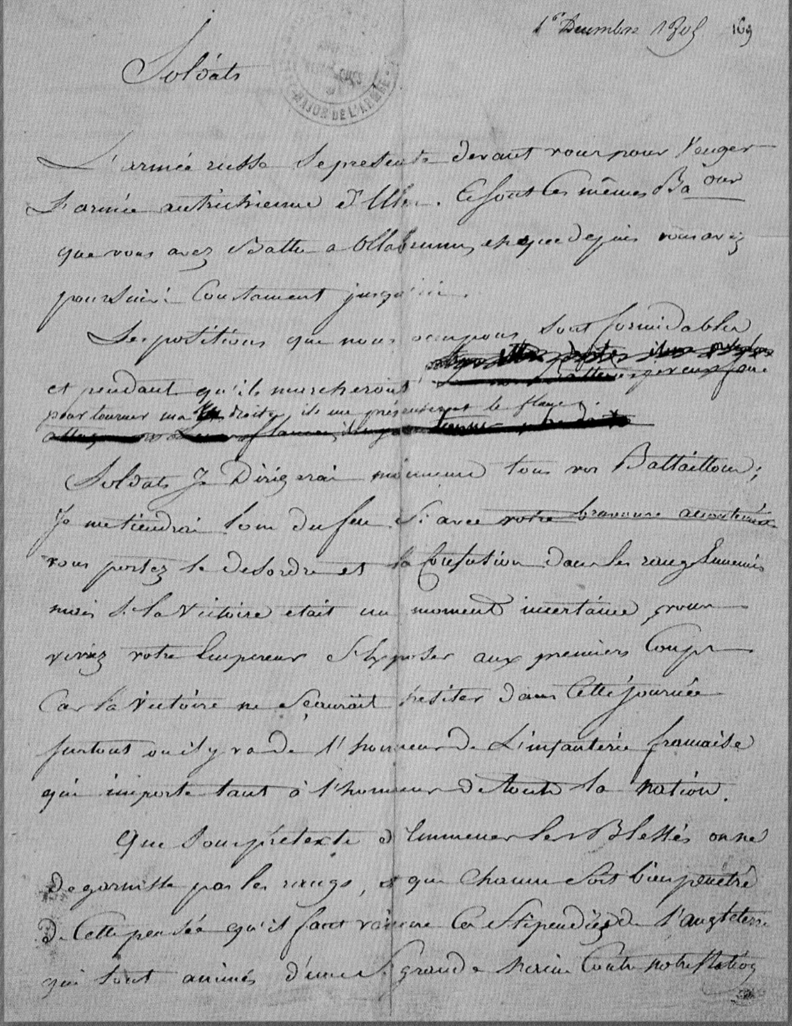

# Napoleon's proclamation to his troops, 1 December 1805

Before the battle of Austerlitz, Napoleon addressed his men.

**Translation**

December 1, 1805

Soldiers,

The Russian Army is confronting us in order to avenge the Austrian Army of Ulm. These are the same battalions that you defeated at Hollabrunn and that you have been pursuing ever since.

The positions we are occupying are formidable, and while they march you should turn to the right, then they will present me with their flank.

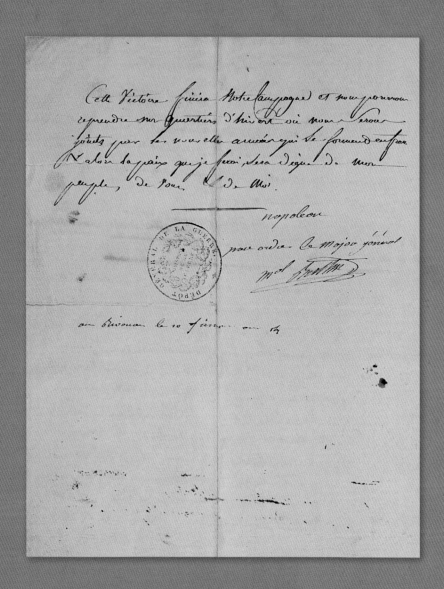

Soldiers, I will direct all your battalions myself. I will keep far away from the fighting if you, with your customary gallantry, bring disorder and confusion into the enemy's ranks, but if victory is for a moment uncertain, you will see your Emperor expose himself to the first blows, because victory cannot hesitate on this day. Let us go where the honour of the French infantry takes us, which is the honour of the whole nation.

Let us not diminish our ranks under the pretext of removing the wounded. May each one of us be consumed with the desire to vanquish these English mercenaries who bear such great hatred for our nation. This victory will end our campaign and we shall be able to return to our former position where we will be joined by new armies currently forming in France. Then the peace which I shall win will be worthy of my people, of you and of me.

Napoleon

On 14 November 1805 Napoleon entered the Austrian capital preceded by Masséna's men. He was then given the keys to the city by the authorities. The only absentee was the Austrian emperor: he had left his palace in Schönbrunn to meet Tsar Alexander, who had demonstrated his support by committing troops.

172

Soldats

Je suis content de vous. vous avez à la journée d'Austerlitz justifié tout ce que j'attendais de votre intrépidité. vous avez décoré vos aigles d'une immortelle gloire. Une armée de cent mille hommes commandée par les Empereurs de Russie et d'Autriche a été en moins de quatre heures ou coupée ou dispersée. Ce qui a échappé à votre fer s'est noyé dans les lacs. 40 drapeaux, les étendards de la Garde impériale de Russie, 120 pièces de canon, vingt généraux, plus de trente mille ~~hommes~~ prisonniers sont le résultat de cette journée à jamais célèbre. Cette infanterie tant vantée et en nombre supérieur n'a pu résister à votre choc, et désormais vous n'avez plus de rivaux à redouter. ainsi en deux mois cette troisième coalition a été vaincue et dissoute. La paix ne peut plus être éloignée, mais, comme je l'ai promis à mon peuple, avant de passer le Rhin, je ne ferai qu'une paix qui nous donne des garanties et assure des récompenses à nos alliés.

Soldats, lorsque le peuple français plaça sur ma tête

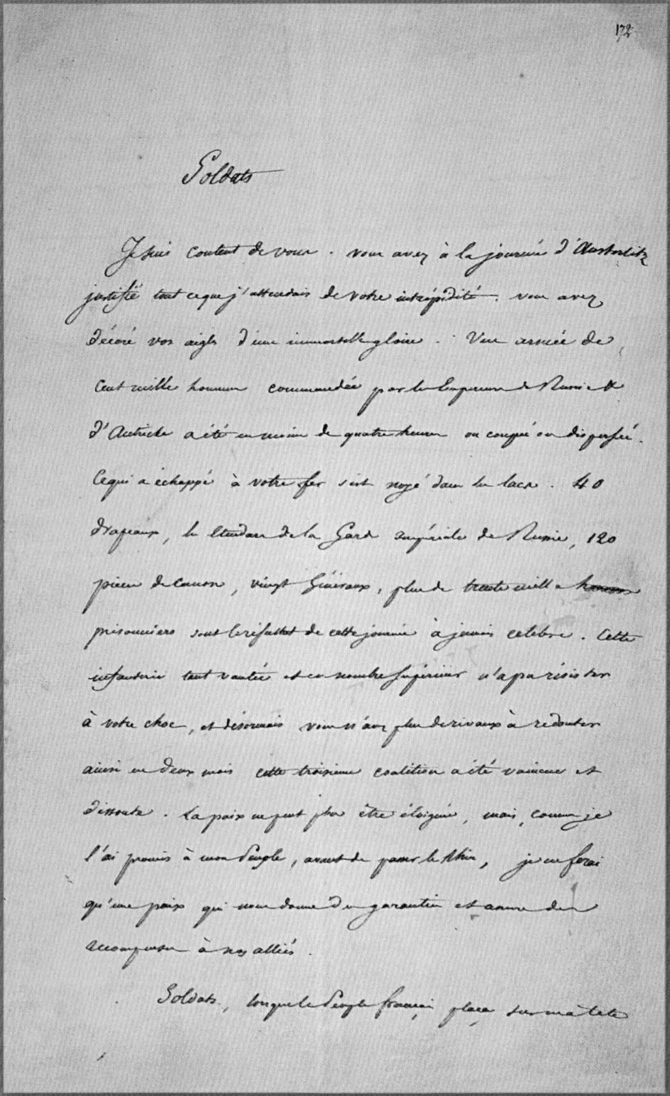

# Napoleon's letter of congratulation to his men after victory at Austerlitz

**Translation**

Dec. 3, 1805

Soldiers,

I am pleased with you. On the day of Austerlitz you justified everything that I expected from your intrepidness. You have adorned your eagles in immortal glory. An army of 100,000 men commanded by the Emperors of Russia and Austria was cut down or dispersed in less than four hours.

Whoever escaped your fire drowned in the lakes. Forty flags, the standards of the Imperial Russian Guard, 120 cannons, 20 generals, more than 30,000 prisoners are the result of this day that will be forever famous. Their much-vaunted infantry was superior in numbers but was incapable of resisting your assault and from now on you have no more rivals to fear, and in two months this third coalition has been beaten and dissolved. Peace can no longer be far away, but as I promised my people before crossing the Rhine, I shall only make a peace that gives me a guarantee and assurances of rewards for our allies.

Soldiers, when the French people placed the imperial crown upon my head, I trusted in you to always maintain this radiant glory, that in my eyes is the only prize. But at the very moment when our enemies thought to destroy it and bring it down, this crown of iron won with the blood of so many Frenchmen, they wanted to force me to place it on the head of your cruellest enemies, a rash and reckless project, which on the very day of the anniversary of you Emperor's coronation, you destroyed and overcame. You taught them that it is easier to face us and threaten us than to beat us.

Soldiers, when all that is necessary to ensure the happiness and prosperity of our homeland has been accomplished, I shall bring you back to France; there, you will be the subject of my warmest congratulations. Your people will see you again with great joy and all you will need to say is: I was at the battle of Austerlitz, for them to reply: here is a brave man.

From our Imperial camp
Austerlitz, 12 Frimaire, year 14

were withdrawing, but in fact the bonfires, which might have been interpreted as the burning of the French camps, had only been lit to celebrate the first anniversary of Napoleon's coronation.

On 2 December, Napoleon allowed the allies to take the initiative. While the right wing resisted the attacks, in the centre, Marshal Soult was ordered to seize the plateau of Pratzen which dominated the battlefield. They took advantage of the fog to conceal this plan of action, and then, when the famous "sun of Austerlitz" appeared, the French attacked the Austro-Russian forces from the rear. In the afternoon, having failed to force their way through to the south, the coalition troops were obliged to withdraw in total disorder, notably towards the Satschan lakes. Davout took up position again in Telnitz and Sokolnitz, Soult continued his wheeling movement on the right, while Bernadotte attacked the Russian Imperial Guard reserves of the Grand Duke Constantine. The death toll was considerable, but of the 15,000 killed or wounded and 20,000 taken prisoner, only 1,290 dead and 6,943 wounded were French.

In the evening, after the battle, Napoleon addressed his troops in front of the Castle of Austerlitz:

"Soldiers, I am pleased with you. On the day of Austerlitz, you justified everything I was expecting of your intrepidity; you have adorned your eagles with immortal glory. … Soldiers, when everything necessary to guarantee the happiness and prosperity of our fatherland has been accomplished, I will take you back to France; there you will be the object of my most tender care. My people will receive you with joy, you will only have to say, 'I was at the battle of Austerlitz' and they will reply, 'There is a brave man'."

Despite the departure of the Russians, the Treaty of Pressburg was signed with the Emperor of Austria a few days later. When the soldiers of the Grande Armée returned to Paris, many monuments were erected in their honour to celebrate the prestigious victory, including the Arc de Triomphe du Carrousel, the Church of la Madeleine and, most notably, the Arc de Triomphe at the Étoile, which was not completed until thirty years later.

**Opposite:** *The mass lighting of candles by the French army was interpreted by the enemy coalition as preparation for a retreat, but in fact the candles marked the celebration of the first anniversary of the emperor's coronation. The glowing sky presaged the confrontations of the next day, which would decide the fate of Europe for the coming decade.*

**Left:** *Napoleon's meeting with Francis two days after the battle, anticipating the Treaty of Pressburg, brought an end to the fighting between their forces. Only Tsar Alexander, the third in this battle of three emperors, refused to bring an end to hostilities.*

**Below:** *This monumental painting by François Gérard shows the crucial moment of General Rapp's presentation of the defeated Grand Duke Constantine and his mounted Russian guards who had been taken prisoner. The sun casts its light on the final skirmishes under Napoleon's majestic gaze.*

## Francis II of Habsburg-Lorraine, later Francis I of Austria (1768–1835)

Before becoming Napoleon's father-in-law, Francis had long been an opponent of the man he considered the heir of the Revolution – "the Corsican Ogre". After succeeding his father Leopold II as Holy Roman Emperor and King of Bohemia and Hungary in 1792, in 1797 he was forced to sign the Treaty of Campo Formio, under which he relinquished the Netherlands and Lombardy. Defeated again at Marengo, he signed the Treaty of Lunéville in 1801, under which he lost all his possessions on the left bank of the Rhine. Napoleon's proclamation in 1804 and the subsequent creation of the Confederation of the Rhine obliged Francis to transform Austria into a hereditary empire. The campaign of 1805, culminating in the Treaty of Pressburg, further reduced his possessions, as did the 1809 campaign and the humiliating Treaty of Schönbrunn. Although his daughter Marie-Louise had become Napoleon's second wife in 1810, and despite the fact that he played a part in the Russian campaign two years later, he took up arms against the French again, joining his troops to those of the Allies in 1813 and 1814. Together with his chancellor, Metternich, he organized the Congress of Vienna, which saw Europe divided in a way that would last for forty years.

# Letter from Napoleon to Joséphine, 5 December 1805

This letter from Napoleon to Joséphine announces the end of the Battle of the three Emperors (Austerlitz).

**Translation**

To the Empress, at Munich
Austerlitz, December 5, 1805

I have concluded a truce. The Russians have gone. The battle of Austerlitz is the grandest of all I have fought. Forty-five flags, more than a 150 pieces of cannon, the standards of the Russian Guards, 20 generals, 30,000 prisoners, more than 20,000 slain – a horrible sight.

The Emperor Alexander is in despair, and on his way to Russia. Yesterday, at my bivouac, I saw the Emperor of Germany. We conversed for two hours; we have agreed to make peace quickly.

The weather is not now very bad. At last behold peace restored to the Continent; it is hoped that it is going to be to the world. The English will not know how to face us.

I look forward with much pleasure to the moment when I can once more be near you. My eyes have been rather bad the last two days; I have never suffered from them before.

Adieu, my dear. I am fairly well, and very anxious to embrace you.

Napoleon

# From Jena to Tilsit

The defeat of the Austrians and Russians at the end of 1805 along with the creation of the Confederation of the Rhine weakened the position of Prussia. After a campaign beginning with a number of engagements, including that of Saalfeld where Prince Louis Ferdinand of Prussia was killed, Napoleon advanced towards Jena. At dawn on 14 October his fifth corps attacked the Landgrafenberg, while the fourth and seventh corps opened the way for a violent combined assault on the front and both wings of the enemy.

As at Austerlitz, the troop movements were masked by very thick fog. After a number of fierce engagements, the Prussian vanguard was driven back. Marshal Ney then engaged in a mad cavalry charge past the village of Vierzenheiligen. At the last moment he received unexpected help from Lannes and the combined actions of Augereau and Soult.

The Prussians were then compelled to withdraw to Erfurt in the north in order to cut off the road to Berlin. Nevertheless, Napoleon made his solemn entry into the capital on 27 October 1806. The *Bulletin de la Grande Armée* recounts the

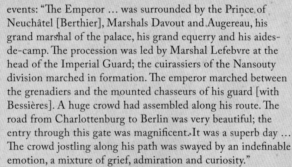

Davout was probably the best strategist close to Napoleon and he participated in all the Grande Armée's campaigns. Having trained at the royal military academies, he fought in the Army of the North and then accompanied Bonaparte to Egypt. When the Empire was proclaimed, he was one of the first to be promoted to marshal. At Austerlitz, it was he who commanded the right wing at Telnitz and Sokolnitz. While Napoleon was defeating the Prussians at Jena, at Auerstedt Davout succeeded in containing the majority of the enemy army commanded by King Frederick William III and the Duke of Brunswick, who died during the course of the battle. Then in 1809, he played a major part in the victories at Eckmuhl and Wagram. As Governor of Prussia, defender of the Duchy of Warsaw and commander of an army corps during the Russian campaign, Davout held out in Germany during the campaigns of 1813 and 1814. He was briefly Minister of War during the Hundred Days.

events: "The Emperor … was surrounded by the Prince of Neuchâtel [Berthier], Marshals Davout and Augereau, his grand marshal of the palace, his grand equerry and his aides-de-camp. The procession was led by Marshal Lefebvre at the head of the Imperial Guard; the cuirassiers of the Nansouty division marched in formation. The emperor marched between the grenadiers and the mounted chasseurs of his guard [with Bessières]. A huge crowd had assembled along his route. The road from Charlottenburg to Berlin was very beautiful; the entry through this gate was magnificent. It was a superb day … The crowd jostling along his path was swayed by an indefinable emotion, a mixture of grief, admiration and curiosity."

Symbolically it was from Berlin that Napoleon issued the decree initiating the Continental System which was intended to prevent Great Britain from trading with the rest of Europe. However, the campaign did not end with this peaceful day, as is evidenced by Lasalle's capture of Stettin and the battles of Pultusk and Golymin.

**Above:** *Less than two weeks after the double victory against the Prussians led by King Frederick Wilhelm, the French marched into Berlin. The Grande Armée's entrance through the Brandeburg Gate instilled fear and respect in a population bowed into submission.*

**Left:** *The Battle of Jena along with the victory at Auerstedt on the same day opened the Grande Armée's way to Berlin. Vernet's painting shows the emperor disrespectfully interrupted while reviewing his troops by one of the grenadiers of his Guard shouting, "Charge!"*

**Right:** *Davout, the real victor of Auerstedt, was undoubtedly one of Napoleon's greatest marshals, as well as the most astute tactician of all the officers of the Empire.*

The Battle of Eylau on 8 February 1807 marked the major turning point of the campaign. The attack of the 6th corps under Augereau was launched first, but they lost their way in a blizzard, and it took the combined intervention of Murat and Dorsenne plus continuous artillery support to keep the Russians at bay. The hand-to-hand fighting was particularly fierce. The arrival of Davout around noon and Ney at the end of the day finished off the action that had begun in the morning. Only the French remained on the battlefield, which had been abandoned by the enemy.

As recorded by Le Moniteur and in a future painting by Gros, the next morning the emperor discovered the extent of the slaughter. "He reviewed several divisions … and visited in turn all the positions that the various French and Russian corps had occupied the day before. The landscape was completely covered with thick snow on which were strewn the bodies of the dead and injured and debris of all kinds of weapons; everywhere traces of blood contrasted with the whiteness of the snow."

The Russians and French now moved into their winter quarters. After a long siege by Lefebvre's troops, lasting from March to May, the city of Danzig capitulated. At the end of spring, the adversaries met again not far from the city of Königsberg (Kaliningrad), at Friedland on the banks of the Alle.

"Of all the imperial battles, Friedland is perhaps the only one that can be compared with Austerlitz in the simplicity and precision of the plan, the fortunate way it developed and the importance of the outcome. It is the very model of a defensive or positional battle, using an improvised formation on terrain assessed at a glance. Both were certainly among the most deliberate and, so to speak, 'manoeuvred' engagements that the emperor conducted. However, the moral importance of the day exceeded its tactical value."

On the morning of 14 June 1807, the "anniversary" of Marengo, Lannes, with around 10,000 soldiers, was keeping the enemy's 50,000 men at bay as they attempted to cross the river. Napoleon had time to send him reinforcements and to prepare a wheeling attack with Ney, who was attacking Bennigsen on the right, and Mortier, who had been posted at Heinrichsdorf. The general attack was launched at five o'clock in the evening, supported by the artillery under Sénarmont and the first corps under Victor, who destroyed the bridges and denied the Russians any possibility of retreat. The confrontation had finally turned in favour of the Grande Armée.

All that remained was to sign a peace treaty with the Russians. The first words spoken by Tsar Alexander on 25 June 1807

**Right:** *This canvas painted by Gros shows all the horror of the Eylau battlefield. The day after the fighting the emperor is shown comforting the wounded, particularly Tsar Alexander's Russian and Lithuanian soldiers.*

– "I hate the English as much as you" – said it all. On a raft anchored in the middle of the River Niemen, the two emperors and former enemies agreed to divide the world between them. Here, over 130 years before the Yalta conference of 1945, unconstrained discussions began regarding the division of territories and zones of influence for each of the sovereigns. Marshals Berthier, Bessières, Murat and Ney and the Grand Duke Constantine, who had been enemies since Austerlitz, faced one another across the river. The peace treaty was signed on 7 July 1807.

"The Emperor of Russia and I have become very close friends and I hope that our political arrangements will henceforth work in harmony," said Bonaparte, after confirming the agreements. From a strictly diplomatic point of view, victory appeared complete. In his speech to the Legislature on 17 August,

Napoleon uttered these words, which made a deep impression on French opinion: "Since your last session, new wars, new triumphs and new peace treaties have changed the political face of Europe. … Our new relationship with Russia has been cemented by the mutual esteem of these two great nations. In everything I have done, my only aim has been the happiness of my peoples, which is dearer to me than my personal glory."

One important point he made was that two days after the conclusion of an agreement with the tsar, a treaty was also signed with the King of Prussia. But in reality the situation with Prussia was quite different. Together with his Russian opposite number, Napoleon had already determined the fate of the third power that had participated in the war of 1807. The King of Saxony, a loyal ally of Napoleon, emerged victorious from the territorial and diplomatic reorganization; he became the new protector of the Grand Duchy of Warsaw, combining the virtues of being a Catholic (indispensable for Poland) and even more importantly a member of the Confederation of the Rhine. In exchange, Napoleon's brother Jerome became King of Westphalia, a state created from parts of Brunswick, the Electorate of Hesse and several other previously autonomous territories. Above all, Berlin and many Prussian provinces remained under French occupation for many months.

This did not prevent Napoleon from welcoming the Queen of Prussia – the wife of Frederick William III, who had urged his subjects to take up arms against the French – to Tilsit. Their meeting became an occasion of mutual delight. The French emperor succeeded in making himself attractive in the eyes of the beautiful Louise, and she considered that "his whole person is reminiscent of a Roman emperor". As for Napoleon he did not hesitate to admit that, as he wrote to Joséphine, "the Queen of Prussia is really charming, she is very flirtatious with me. But don't be jealous, it all runs off me like water off a duck's back. It would cost me too much to act like a suitor."

## Alexander I of Russia (1777–1825)

The beginning of Alexander's reign was marked by the brutal assassination of his father, Paul I, who was strangled in 1801. He immediately relaunched the anti-French coalition and participated in the military campaigns but suffered defeat at Austerlitz, and after Eylau he was forced to come to agreement with Napoleon at Tilsit and Erfurt. Deeply influenced by religion, he was sure he could refuse Napoleon's offers. Thanks to his wait-and-see policy, he finally forced the Grande Armée to retreat from his territory and twice defeated the last faint hopes of his enemy on the battlefields of Saxony and France. A close friend of the Beauharnais family, at the Congress of Vienna he had a decisive influence in easing the conditions that his allies demanded should be imposed on the fallen emperor.

**Above:** *Long suspected of having ordered the death of his father Paul I, Tsar Alexander had a strange relationship with Napoleon, the man whom he would consider successively as "the Usurper" up until 1807, his "friend" after the meeting in Tilsit, and then "the Antichrist" after the Russian campaign.*

# The Peninsular War

After the pact with Russia, Napoleon turned his attention to attempting to destroy the British economy. He demanded that other countries suppress trade with his enemy and deny their ports to British ships, but this was opposed by Spain and Portugal. After the Battle of Trafalgar, France and Spain, which had been allies until then, especially at sea, found themselves on opposite sides.

On 29 November 1807, General Junot's troops arrived in Spain. More than 50,000 men were sent to the Lisbon area, which was still one of the hubs of trade with Britain. After the fall of Portugal, Murat took control of Madrid on 23 March 1808 with a force of 100,000 soldiers.

The Spanish kings Charles IV and his son Ferdinand VII – Ferdinand had succeeded to the throne after the forced abdication of his father – were summoned to Bayonne to hand over power to Napoleon. While they were there a popular uprising broke out in Madrid on 2 May 1808. This was triggered by the hasty departure of the king's daughter, the ex-queen of Etruria, and his son, the Infante Francisco de Paula, whose removal had been ordered by Napoleon. The rioters rushed to the royal palace, which the two heirs of the Bourbons were being forced to leave. One of Murat's aides-de-camp, the head of the Lagrange squadron, was the first victim of the violence which was led by Molina and the officers Daioz and Velarde. In order to suppress the 20,000 or so citizens of Madrid involved in this action, Murat sent in reinforcements, including a platoon of Mamelukes who went straight to the Puerta del Sol. They were met by the bullets and knives of the insurgents, and Mustapha, one of the heroes of Austerlitz, was killed. As a result, the hand-to-hand fighting became fiercer than ever. As recounted by Marbot, "on witnessing the arrival of the Mamelukes, whom they greatly feared, the Spaniards nevertheless attempted to

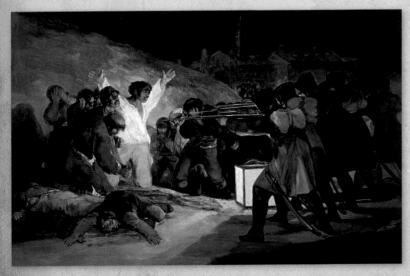

**Opposite below left:** *The second part of Goya's diptych dealing with the 2 May uprising and the cold-hearted executions of the following day marked a turning point in Spanish national consciousness. The work would have a great impact on the Romantics and its influence can be discerned in Manet's* The Death of Maximilian *and Picasso's* Guernica.

**Below:** *The crossing of the Somosierra Pass was one of the greatest military achievements of the French cavalry. The sacrifice of the Poles in the vanguard opened up the road to Madrid for the emperor and his troops. Madrid surrendered on 4 December.*

# Francisco José de Goya y Lucientes (1746–1828)

Although he at first sided with King Joseph and retained his position as court painter, Goya became a fierce opponent of Napoleonic power after Ferdinand's restoration to the throne in 1814. This change of attitude is symbolized by the paintings *The Second of May 1808* and *The Third of May 1808*. Goya had a precocious talent and was taught by the neoclassical painter Mengs. After a stay in Rome, he led a turbulent life before entering the service of the King of Spain in Madrid. He was talented in many areas; his skill, speed of execution and flashes of brilliance resulted in the creation of dozens of portraits, groups and bullfighting scenes. He became the most famous painter in Europe of the early nineteenth century and his modernism would inspire several generations of artists right up to Picasso.

**Above:** *Goya's unflattering portraits of the Spanish monarchy and his hallucinatory visions of war made him one of the principal standard bearers of European Romanticism.*

resist; but their resolve was short-lived, as even the bravest were terrified by the sight of the Turks."

The suppression that followed the next day, still under the leadership of Murat, was ruthless, and Napoleon approved, saying, "I am very pleased with the force you used." Execution squads were stationed on the hill of Principe Pio, at the Prado and even outside some of the churches.

A violent six-year struggle then began between the French, who were determined that the throne of Spain should be given to Joseph Bonaparte (Napoleon's brother, who would leave the throne of Naples to his brother-in-law Murat), and the Spanish, supported by the British troops. At the head of 18,000 men, Dupont de l'Etang was forced to surrender at Bailén in July 1808. After the defeat of Junot by the forces of the Duke of Wellington in late August in Portugal, and the defeat and eviction of the French troops there, Napoleon decided to go to Madrid as quickly as possible to help Murat. But the route to Madrid ran through the Somosierra Pass, which was defended by a force of 13,000 men under the command of Don Benito San Juan. The four bends in the road were the scene of a dramatic episode, in which the intrepid Montbrun and Kozietulski's 500 Polish Light Cavalry distinguished themselves.

The Count of Ségur would long remember this episode, which has gone down in posterity as an example of total sacrifice:

"We must have encountered 40,000 shots and more than twenty rounds of grapeshot per minute! ... Any other force would have hesitated, but with these heroic Poles there was no sign. I hardly had time to draw my sword from its scabbard, when they began to charge in a column along the road. We charged at top speed. ... But the enemy fire was too accurate! Almost the entire squadron was felled. Of the other six officers, three more were killed outright or mortally wounded ... . Forty non-commissioned officers and lancers, killed or mortally wounded, lay strewn on the ground. Twelve others were wounded, but less seriously; only twenty escaped this massacre safe and sound. These last had gone to help their wounded comrades to retreat; so the only person I saw standing on the ground over which we had charged was a single bugler."

On 4 December 1808, Napoleon was present at the surrender of Madrid. But for all that, the fires of resistance had not been extinguished, as the two successive sieges of Saragossa proved. Joseph Bonaparte, who had never really been accepted by the Spanish and had been nicknamed "Pepe Botella" (because he was accused of being a drunkard and not caring about the fate of his subjects), but who had nevertheless been restored to the

throne, witnessed the arrival of the British in the Peninsula. His troops were defeated at Salamanca in July 1812, and again on 21 June 1813 at Vitoria, at the hands of Wellington's British army. The French were forced to retreat over the Pyrenees, and the campaign ended in a complete rout, aggravated in part by the dissension between Marshals Soult, Suchet, Ney and Masséna.

**Opposite:** *Despite fighting relentlessly to put his brother Joseph on the Spanish throne, Napoleon is here depicted showing mercy to the Spanish insurgents after their capital had fallen into the hands of French soldiers.*

**Left:** *History recalls the long Siege of Zaragoza as hand-to-hand fighting between heroic defenders and courageous attackers, but in fact the French soldiers needed two attempts to quell the city's fierce resistance.*

**Below:** *After their defeat at Astorga at the hands of Soult's men, Moore's Englishmen are presented to the emperor as a long line of prisoners. At this point most of the enemy forces had retreated.*

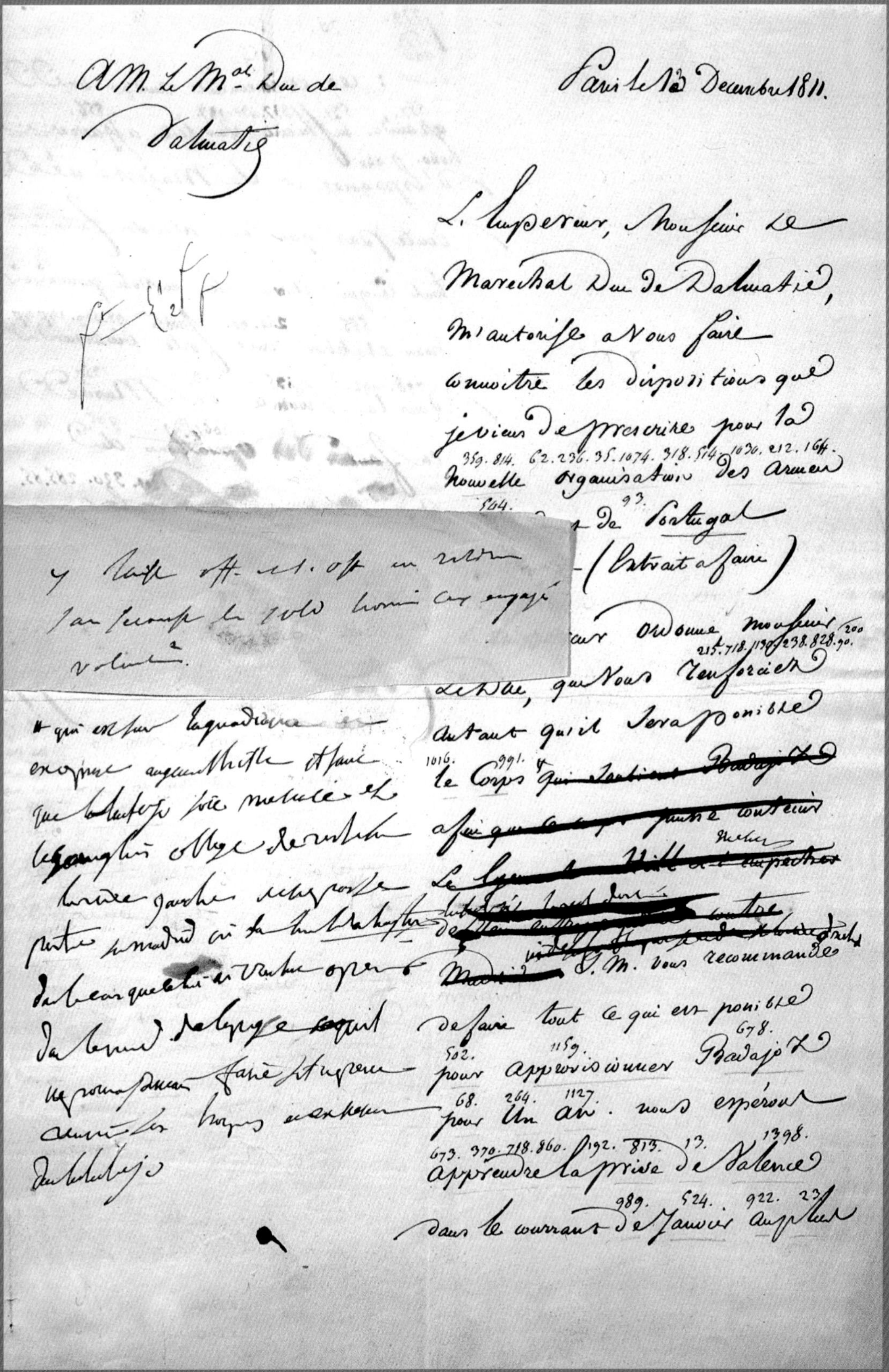

À M. Le M.al Duc de
Dalmatie

Paris le 13 Décembre 1811.

L'Empereur, Monsieur le
Maréchal Duc de Dalmatie,
m'autorise à vous faire
connoître les dispositions que
je viens de prescrire pour la
359. 814. 62. 236. 35. 1074. 318. 514. 1036. 212. 164.
nouvelle organisation des armées
504.                    93.
                de Portugal
                        ( Extrait à faire )

                                        200
                        215. 718. 130. 238. 828. 90.
            ... ordonne Monsieur
    ... que vous renforciés
    autant qu'il sera possible
1016.   991. &
le Corps qui attient ~~Badajoz~~

~~...~~

~~...~~ S.M. vous recommande
de faire tout ce qui est possible
    502.      1159.          678.
pour approvisionner Badajoz ~~&~~
    68.   264.     1127.
pour un an. nous espérons
673. 370. 718. 860. 192. 813. 13.  1398.
apprendre la prise de Valence
            989.   524.  922.  23/
dans le courant de Janvier au plus

[margin note:]
y laisse off. et s. off en retour
... beaucoup de vols hommes ... engagé
volont.

[left column lower:]
... qui est sur l'escadrière ...
... augmentée ... et faire
que ... votre mesure ...
... oblige de ...
... jusqu'à Madrid où la ...
de beaucoup de ... vente ouverte
de ... Salpye ... qui
... faire ...
... les hommes ...
...

# Order to defend Madrid, 1811

By means of this document dated 13 December 1811, written in his own hand, Napoleon gave Soult the order to defend the City of Madrid.

**Translation**

To Marshall [Soult] Duke of Dalmatia1
Paris 13th December 1811

*(Text on right of page)*
To Marshall [Soult] Duke of Dalmatia, the Emperor grants me permission to tell you about the arrangements that I have stipulated for the re-organisation of the armies (text hidden under superimposed paper) ... of Portugal (more text hidden ) then: (Excerpt to be done)
(more text hidden) ... order Marshall [Soult], that you reinforce as much as possible the Corps
[which defends Badajoz so that the Corps might be able hold General ... and prevent him...]3 .... (rest of words crossed out and not legible). H. M. (His Majesty) enjoins you to do your utmost to provide Badajoz with enough supplies to last for a year. We hope to learn of the
capture of Valence sometime in January at the latest.

*(Text on left of page is thought to be by Napoleon himself although it is illegible.)*

# The Austrian Campaign

Having just returned from Madrid, Napoleon was now forced to send the major part of his forces towards Austria. This followed Austria's invasion of Bavaria, an ally of France, on 9 April 1809. While the Tyrol rose in rebellion, Prince Eugène was forced to retreat after the Battle of Sacile. Between 19 and 23 April, Napoleon rescued the situation, defeating the Austrian troops at Teugen-Hausen, Abensberg, Landshut, Eckmuhl and Ratisbon. At the same time, Marshal Lefebvre regained control of Innsbruck which had fallen into the hands of the insurgents led by Andreas Hofer.

As the bridges in Vienna across the Danube had been destroyed, Napoleon's army was obliged to rebuild them before it could even think of confronting the troops of Archduke Charles. On 21 May 1809, the men commanded by Masséna and Lannes, having taken the villages of Aspern and Essling on the far bank of the river, had been attacked by the Austrians but kept their positions. The next day, Napoleon supported them with his Guard, the Oudinot corps and almost his entire cavalry, while Davout remained on the other bank. But in the middle of the day, after ordering an attack on the enemy's centre, the emperor was forced to retreat to the island of Lobau in the middle of the Danube. There were significant losses on both sides, but the French were most saddened by the fatal wounding of Marshal Lannes.

It then took six weeks to take care of the troops and more importantly to wait for reinforcements. This time, it was not two bridges but eight that were magically provided, three of which

Born in the same year as Napoleon, Lannes enlisted in the second battalion of the Gers Volunteers at Auch and then participated in the campaign in the Eastern Pyrenees between 1793 and 1795. His bravery was noticed by his superiors and General Bonaparte, especially after the Italian campaign and the Battle of Dego. At Lodi, Arcole and Rivoli, no effort was spared. In Egypt, he captured El Arich, distinguished himself at the Siege of Acre in May 1798 and fought victoriously at Aboukir, becoming brigadier-general shortly afterwards. After Marengo, he commanded the Consular Guard and then became ambassador to Portugal. He was created Marshal of the Empire in 1804, participated in the major battles of the Empire (Austerlitz, Jena, Friedland) and led the troops in Spain, but in 1809 he lost his life a few days after Essling. Napoleon, devastated by the news, is said to have declared, "In Lannes, courage at first prevailed over intellect; but the intellect grew each day until the two were equal; I took him on as a pygmy, I have lost a giant."

served to decoy their Austrian opponents. The long days also afforded Napoleon the opportunity to visit wounded soldiers.

Despite a violent storm that threatened to sweep away all the recently completed building work, the battle was joined on 5 July in the neighbourhood of Deutsch-Wagram. Though the fighting was intense, the soldiers persevered with their efforts for forty-eight hours, as the attempt to cross the Austrian line at Rüssbach eventually failed.

Conditions were different on the morning of 6 July and threw the emperor's plans into complete disarray. Marshal Bessières, in command of the cavalry, was wounded. Napoleon had to act quickly to propose a new strategy to his men if he was to thwart the offensive of Archduke Charles. At the same time as the initial troop movements, a long column of 67,000 men was formed and the signal to engage was given shortly before midday. With crossed bayonets, the men advanced, supported by a battery of 100 cannons ceaselessly bombarding the enemy positions.

The breakthrough was successful and the order was given for a general offensive. All the superior officers were involved. Even Marshal Masséna continued to lead his men to victory, despite the fact that he had been ill for three days. He was transported to the

*Opposite: It was during the capture of Ratisbonne, where Lannes distinguished himself yet again, that Napoleon was hit by a bullet for the first time. He was wounded in the heel but was immediately treated by the surgeon Yvan. Napoleon then went straight back to the battlefield, where his reappearance galvanized the troops.*

*Above: The Battle of Essling, an especially bloody affair, served as the stage for a drama that was both personal and symbolic. Here the emperor's faithful friend, Marshal Lannes, lies fatally wounded in front of him. Lannes would die a few days later in Keiserebersdorf, not far from Vienna, on 31 May 1809.*

*Right: Lannes was not only one of Napoleon's most courageous officers but also one of his closest companions. He was involved in all the battles after the First Italian Campaign.*

battlefield in his carriage and was at the very centre of events. His courage commanded the admiration of his companions in the 4th corps and won the respect of his enemies. However, although the victory was finally won, Masséna would later recall that, despite all the effort spent, "after so many labours and clever manoeuvres, the emperor was astonished to reap no greater reward than that of winning the victory and the fruitless honour of sleeping on the battlefield."

Archduke Charles signed the armistice after the Battle of Znaim on 10 and 11 July, and then Emperor Francis I signed the Treaty of Schönbrunn on 14 October 1809. With the exception of Spain, Europe was finally at peace. France, which stretched from Barcelona to Hamburg and from Antwerp to Ljubljana (then known as Laibach), was now composed of 130 départements.

"Any hussar who is not dead by the age of thirty is a blackguard." With his characteristic ability for a neat turn of phrase and a certain love of provocation common to all hussars, General Lasalle was bound to please Napoleon. His career began during the Revolution, and he very soon achieved the rank of captain in 1796 followed by exploits in Italy and Egypt. He was made a commander of the Legion of Honour when the order was first created, and achieved considerable successes in Austria and especially in Prussia. On 29 October 1806, he forced the surrender of Stettin and watched the 6,000 or so men who had defended the city file past his 500 hussars. He then distinguished himself in the fighting at Golymin and Heilsberg, and again in Spain at Somosierra and Medellin.

Without delay he was recalled by the emperor, who had just begun a new campaign in Austria, and arrived in Vienna on 19 May 1809. Three days later, he played a brilliant part in the Battle of Essling. In early July during the Battle of Wagram, Lasalle, despite suffering from exhaustion, courageously took command of the Cuirassiers de Saint-Sulpice. Forgetting that they did not charge as fast as the hussars, he found himself alone ahead of all his horsemen and was struck in the forehead by a bullet. The night before Lasalle had written to his wife, "My heart is for you, my blood for the emperor and my life for honour."

**Opposite above:** *By sharing his soldiers' everyday life and sleeping in the open on the battlefield, Napoleon projected the image of the "little corporal" who rested only when obliged to.*

**Left:** *By daybreak Napoleon would be astride his white charger, directing manoeuvres and placing himself in danger. The defeat of the Austrians at Wagram was one of his most resounding victories, where he was ably assisted by his battle-hardened marshals and soldiers.*

**Above:** *Lasalle, who specialized in leading his hussars in cavalry charges, was struck down at the Battle of Wagram. He was hit by a bullet to the head while giving chase to the Hungarians. The night before he had found his famous pipe broken; seeing this as a premonition, he mournfully predicted his death.*

# Divorce and Remarriage

**O**n 12 October 1809, when Napoleon was watching the parade of the Guard at the castle of Schönbrunn, a young man named Friedrich Staps was arrested. He was carrying a knife and made no bones about admitting that his intention had been to assassinate the emperor. Napoleon was aware that he was always at the mercy of a fanatic's dagger, or a Russian or Austrian bullet. With no direct heir, what would happen if he were to die? Who would succeed him? At the time of his coronation, he had made his nephews and his stepson Eugène possible heirs to the crown. "But Eugène does not bear my name," he sighed. "After me, there would be complete anarchy."

For a long time, Napoleon believed he was incapable of fathering children. After all, Joséphine had twice been a mother at the time of their marriage. But after the birth of his illegitimate child Count Léon, he realized that he could have a legitimate heir. From that time on, reasons of State prevailed over his attachment to the woman who had been the companion of his youthful glory and the driving force behind his meteoric rise. Napoleon decided to separate from Joséphine. He announced the dreadful news to his step-daughter Hortense. "I have made up my mind. It is irrevocable. The whole of France wants this divorce; the people are crying aloud for it. I cannot oppose their wishes. So nothing will make me change my mind, neither tears nor prayers."

On 30 November at Fontainebleau, Napoleon informed Joséphine of his decision. She had been prepared for it for a long time, as the question of divorce had constantly arisen since November 1807, and all the more so because on 10 June 1809 Pope Pius VII had excommunicated the emperor in the bull *Quem Memorando* following the union of Rome and the Papal States with the French Empire.

Joséphine fainted, or pretended to; Baron de Bausset, the emperor's chamberlain, ran over and took her in his arms to lift her up. Though the weakness may have been faked, her grief was nonetheless sincere. As for Napoleon, he confided to one of his close friends, "I am even more saddened by the scene Joséphine has just made. I am deeply sorry for her, but I thought she had more character and I was not prepared for her outbursts of grief."

The members of the Bonaparte family were delighted by the news because they at last saw the dismissal of the woman they had always thought of as a schemer. In 1804, they had tried every means to prevent the coronation of the pretty Créole woman whom they still looked upon as a "woman of easy virtue".

The divorce, or rather the dissolution of the marriage, was pronounced on 14 December 1809. Napoleon, trying to conceal his emotion, declared, "Far from ever having had reason to complain, on the contrary I have nothing but praise for the affection and tenderness of my beloved wife. … She was crowned by my hand; I wish her to keep the rank and title of empress, and I particularly wish that she may never

doubt my feelings and will always consider me as her best and dearest friend." Next, Joséphine tried to read the text of the renunciation that she had drawn up herself, but because her throat was constricted through sorrow she could not manage it and passed the pages to Regnault de Saint-Jean-d'Angély to read out. The chateau of Malmaison became her place of exile. In fact, Napoleon granted her the same status as a dowager empress, with an annual pension of two million francs. She kept her court and the Château de Navarre, near Evreux, was put at her disposal.

For Napoleon the priority was now to marry as soon as possible to ensure the succession of the dynasty. A private meeting was held on 21 January 1810 and three potential fiancées were short-listed: Maria Augusta, Princess of Saxony; the Russian Grand Duchess, Anna Pavlovna, the youngest sister of Tsar Alexander I; and the Austrian Archduchess Marie-Louise of Habsburg-Lorraine. After a few days, the latter was finally chosen and she was forced for reasons of state to accept marriage with the "Corsican Ogre". Napoleon delegated his

## Marie Walewska (1786–1817)

When Napoleon, who was on his way from Pultusk to Warsaw, and Marie Walewska met at a coaching inn at Bronie, she changed the life of the emperor. The eldest daughter of a noble family, she had married Count Anastase Walewski, chamberlain to the last king of Poland and fifty years her senior. She had nurtured an enduring hatred of the Russians since the death of her father. She became Napoleon's mistress and confidante, imagining that he would restore Poland's dignity and the lands that had been dismembered by her powerful neighbour. In May 1810 Marie gave birth to Napoleon's son Alexandre and settled in Paris for a time. After the first abdication in April 1814 she hastened to Fontainebleau, but was unable to see the emperor. In September the same year, she went to the island of Elba to offer him comfort, arriving unexpectedly in the middle of the night and accompanied by their little son. After these two days of emotional and romantic reunion, their final meeting took place on 26 June 1815 at Malmaison, a few days before Napoleon's departure for St Helena.

**Above:** *In the course of just a few weeks, Napoleon separated from Joséphine by obtaining the official dissolution of their union and found a new fiancée in the shape of the Archduchess Marie-Louise. Although Joséphine was deeply saddened and hurt, she was resigned to the fact that she could not provide Napoleon's much-desired heir.*

**Left:** *The dissolution was arranged in March 1810 and Napoleon, having first considered one of the Tsar's sisters, would finally marry the Austrian princess by proxy in Vienna. On 27 March the young bride finally met Napoleon and made her appearance on his arm in Compiègne.*

**Right:** *In May 1910, while all of Europe was still talking about the emperor's remarriage, Marie Walewska, his Polish mistress, gave him a son. She received a gift of Brussels lace for the boy, Alexandre, who forty years later would become a minister under his blood cousin Napoleon III.*

## Letter from Joséphine, 1809

By means of this document, the Empress Joséphine consented "to a sacrifice [...] for the good of the country" and agreed to divorce Napoleon, who would go on to marry the Archduchess Marie-Louise.

### Translation

With the permission of (?) our august and dear husband, I must acknowledge that I was still harbouring the hope of having children who would have satisfied the political needs and interests of France, it gives me pleasure to give him the highest proof of attachment and devotion that could ever be given on this earth. I owe him so much kindness, I was crowned by his hand, and from the height of this throne, I have received nothing but tokens of affection and love from the French people.

bonheur d'être un jour gouvernée
par les descendants d'un grand
homme si évidemment suscité
par la providence pour effacer
les maux d'une terrible révolution
et rétablir l'autel, le trône et
l'ordre social, mais la dissolution
de mon mariage ne changera
rien aux sentiments de mon
cœur : l'empereur aura toujours
en moi sa meilleure amie.
je sais combien cet acte commandé
par la politique et par de si
grands intérêts, a froissé son
cœur ; mais l'un et l'autre
nous sommes glorieux du sacrifice
que nous faisons au bien de la
patrie. ❦ joséphine

These are my feelings when consenting to the dissolution of a marriage which from
now on would have been a hindrance to the good of France, which would have
deprived it of the happiness of being one day governed by the descendants of a great
man so obviously provided by providence to erase the memory of a terrible revolution
and to re-establish the altar, the throne and heavenly order. But the dissolution of my
marriage will not change the sentiments of my heart: the emperor will always have in
me his best friend. I know how much this action, driven by politics and for the sake of
higher interests, has bruised his heart; but he and I are both glorious in a sacrifice that
we are making for the good of the fatherland.

Joséphine

# Invitation to Napoleon's second marriage

Invitation, issued by the services of the master of ceremonies, to the celebration of the marriage of Napoleon and Marie-Louise in the Louvre, April 1810.

**Translation**

*Front:*

Marriage ceremony

of

His Majesty the Emperor Napoleon,

with

H I & R H (Her Imperial and Royal Highness)
the Archduchess

Marie-Louise.

*Reverse:*

Museum Gallery
Entry ticket for one man

Entry will be by way of the two staircases
outside the Pavilion de L'Horloge,
on the Quayside and on the rue des Orties.

Doors will open at seven, and will close at midday.

Men are to wear French dress.

(In the oval stamp: Initials followed by
"Grand Master of Ceremony")

chief-of-staff Berthier to go to Vienna as soon as possible to make the official request for her hand. On 8 March it was a fait accompli. The next day Berthier and the Austrian foreign minister Metternich signed the marriage contract modelled on that of Marie-Antoinette. Two days later, on Sunday 11 March, the religious ceremony took place, by proxy, in St Augustine's Church in Vienna. Napoleon was represented by Archduke Charles.

On 13 March, at eight o'clock in the morning, Marie-Louise left Vienna for Paris. To the sound of bells and the noise of cannon fire, the long convoy of travel coaches set off through the decorated streets. Napoleon, at great expense, had dispatched some of the domestic servants from the palace to Braunau. They were charged with meeting Marie-Louise for the ceremony of exchange by which the young woman would become French, as had happened to Marie-Antoinette in her time.

On 27 March, Napoleon, impatient to meet his new wife, joined the procession even before it reached Compiègne and spent the night with his young bride. Four days later, the new imperial couple went to Saint-Cloud where, on 1 April, the civil wedding was celebrated. The next day, a second religious ceremony was held in the chapel of the Louvre. Less than a year later, on 20 March 1811, the empress gave birth to Napoleon François Charles Joseph Bonaparte. The woman whom Napoleon looked upon as a brood mare had given him the heir he had so eagerly awaited.

**Left:** *On 2 April 1810, Napoleon married Marie-Louise in the presence of the imperial family. The religious ceremony took place in the Salon Carré of the Louvre which was specially redecorated for the occasion. The young bride wore a magnificent dress made of white tulle embroidered with silver designed by the great couturier Leroy. Her shoulders were covered by the same red velvet train that Joséphine had worn at Napoleon's coronation.*

**Below:** *After the ceremony, the imperial couple left for a long honeymoon that took them, most notably, to Anvers where they were honoured by the Belgians.*

## Marie-Louise of Habsburg (1791–1847)

Having been chosen for the position of Archduchess of Austria, in 1810 Marie-Louise married Napoleon, the man whom she had long been taught to regard as the enemy above all others. At their first meeting she immediately showed great willingness to fulfil her role as wife, mother of the future heir and Empress of France (despite the still vivid memory of her aunt, Marie-Antoinette, who had been guillotined by the Revolutionaries seventeen years previously). After twice acting as regent, she returned to Austria with her son and did not see Napoleon again after he left to rejoin his armies in January 1814. After the fall of the Empire, she took the title of Duchess of Parma and remarried the Count of Neipperg.

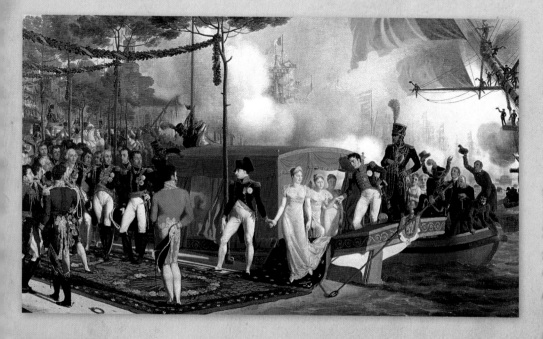

# Moscow and the Retreat from Russia

**T**he interval of peace between France and her monarchist adversaries did not last long. The British never lowered their guard, evident in the barbed comments made on the diplomatic scene, and the flame of nationalism was rekindled on the Iberian peninsula, where British troops supported Spanish resistance.

However, this time the opposition to Napoleon's regime would come from the east. With the Austrians now allied with France and the Prussians still on their knees, it was the Russians who took up the torch. The French emperor had no desire to let them make the first move: "It would be best to wage this war while I have all my strength; I do not wish to leave it to my successor, to a child. After this war, the European system will be founded; the cause of the century will have been won."

The formation of the Grand Duchy of Warsaw under the treaties of 1807 and the obvious impossibility of allowing the tsar to take possession of Constantinople were bound to cause fresh hostilities between Paris and St Petersburg. As Napoleon later said on Saint Helena, "I could have shared the Ottoman Empire with Russia; we discussed it more than once. Constantinople always saved it. This capital was the big problem, the real stumbling block. Russia wanted it; I could not agree. It was too precious a key, worth an empire in itself. Whoever possessed it would be able to rule the world."

Pre-empting an attack that the Russians had been preparing for over a year, Napoleon went to Strasbourg and then to his headquarters at Wilkowyrzki. War was declared on 22 June 1812. He addressed his troops as follows: "Soldiers! The second

Kutuzov, the man whom Tolstoy elevated to an icon in *War and Peace*, had all the qualities of a national hero. In fact the Russian field-marshal had followed a long career in the forces of Catherine II before the episode with Napoleon. Having fought in Poland, Turkey and the Crimea, he lost his right eye in 1773 and was then removed from positions of responsibility for refusing to take part in the plot against Paul I. He only returned to the high command in 1805. It was he who commanded (against his will) the coalition forces defeated at Austerlitz. His hour of glory was undoubtedly the Russian campaign of 1812, in particular the pursuit of the remains of the Grande Armée to the banks of the Berezina. After the triumph in Moldavia, he was made a prince and commander-in-chief of the Russian army, and continued to harass the French. However, he fell victim to septicaemia during the following campaign and died in Silesia in April 1813.

Polish war has begun; the first ended at Friedland and Tilsit. … Russia is the victim of fate! Her destiny must be accomplished. Does she think you are degenerate? Are we no longer the soldiers we were at Austerlitz?" Then he immediately had his men "cross the Rubicon" in the form of the Niemen, which had been considered the boundary between the two zones of influence since the talks at Tilsit. More than 650,000 men made ready to strike at their former ally. Eleven main corps, four cavalry corps and one corps of reserves set off to confront just under a million armed Russians.

Choosing to advance on Moscow rather than forcing Alexander to retreat to St Petersburg quickly proved to be a strategic error. After the Battle of Smolensk, where the Russians refused to engage in the fighting, Napoleon confided, "We have gone too far to retreat. … Peace lies ahead of us; we are only eight days away. So close to our goal, there is no more to discuss. Let us march on Moscow."

The Russian tactic of refusing to join battle continued for several weeks, taking its toll on the organization of the French troops as well as on their nerves. The decisive battle eventually took place on 7 September 1812 against the troops of the aging Kutuzov, whom Napoleon had fought at Austerlitz in 1805. Altogether 260,000 men faced one another, with equal numbers on each side.

The size of the battlefield of Borodino, known to the French as "La Moskowa" – "May people say of you: he was in the great battle below the walls of Moscow!" proclaimed the emperor – was unlike anything the French had encountered previously. Above all, the confrontation between the two huge forces led

**Opposite:** *The city of Smolensk fell to the French on the night of 17 August 1812. In this painting by Langlois, Napoleon is depicted issuing orders alongside Murat. The Russians had no qualms about burning their houses rather than allowing them to fall into French hands.*

**Above:** *The decisive Battle of Borodino allowed the Grand Armée to march on to Moscow, although both sides declared themselves the victors of this confrontation. Lejeune's depiction of the high points of this dramatic battle on one canvas is symptomatic of the inconclusive nature of the events of 7 September 1812. Here we see the fatal wounding of General Caulaincourt, treatment provided by the surgeon, Larrey, and the capture of the Great Redoubt. A week later the French were in the Kremlin.*

to a terrifying, confused and bloody battle that ended without any real victor. To motivate his men, Napoleon showed them a portrait of his son (known as the King of Rome since birth), the future of the Empire. After four hours of fighting, during which 1,200 cannons belched forth, the entire French right outflanked the enemy positions. Caulaincourt's cuirassiers captured the famous Great Redoubt, considered to be the centre of the enemy deployment. Almost a week later, the imperial troops entered Moscow.

But on the evening of 15 September 1812, when the French had taken up quarters in the religious capital of Russia and Napoleon had moved into a suite in the Kremlin, the thousand-year-old city, now empty of all its native inhabitants, went up in flames. On the instructions of Rostopchin, the father of the future Countess of Ségur, people lit fires all over the city which the French were unable to extinguish. As Napoleon later admitted:

"Despite the poetry, all the stories of the burning of Troy were nothing like the reality of Moscow. There was a violent gale blowing, all the pumps had been taken. It was literally a sea of flames. We had marched so quickly and our entry had been so sudden that people had taken nothing with them. The women had fled so hastily that we even found diamonds on their dressing-tables. They commended their property to the loyalty of the victors."

But well before the start of the fire, another misfortune had begun to afflict an army requiring a large quantity of provisions: pillaging was rife and the few foodstuffs available were fast disappearing.

The *Bulletin de la Grande Armée* described Moscow on 16 September such: "...as big as Paris; it is an extremely rich city, filled with the palaces of all the chief citizens of the Empire … There we found considerable resources of every kind." Four days later, the *Bulletin* stated that "the fire in this capital will set Russia back a hundred years". The following day, Napoleon returned to the Kremlin to find that the city was no more than a field of ruin and desolation. The victors had become prisoners of their own capture, as Kutuzov had predicted; "Moscow" he said, "will be the sponge that will soak up the Grande Armée." In addition, Alexander I would not meet to discuss a new treaty. There was no option but to retreat.

From November, everything changed radically. After marching for several weeks, the tail end of the French army endured traumatic suffering. The troops discovered the true nature of the Russian cold, far more dangerous than the enemy soldiers, and gave it the apt name of "General Winter". Travelling back along the same road on which they had advanced east, the army found supplies were extremely limited due to the scorched earth policy pursued by the Russians as they fell back to Moscow.

After the terrible Battle of Krasnoi, where French forces were heavily defeated and lost further supplies, the survivors arrived at the River Berezina. More and more men became cut off, making the task of the officers more complicated. The arrival of Russian troops under Kutuzov, Chichagov and Wittgenstein was imminent. Two bridges thrown across the Berezina close to the village of Studienka were not sufficient to allow the thousands of soldiers who had been fleeing from the Cossacks since Moscow, to cross. Despite the dedication of General Eblé and his pontoniers, who did not hesitate to plunge into the icy

*Opposite above:* *What were Napoleon's thoughts when faced with this sight? Did he, like Nero in Rome, feel responsible for such a terrible cultural catastrophe, with the Kremlin and the suburbs of Moscow in flames? This print by Vereshchagin, a Russian painter who worked in France and admired the emperor, illustrates the complexity of a campaign that marked the beginning of the Grand Armée's decline.*

*Opposite below:* *From 15 to 18 November 1812 the French fought the Battle of Krasnoi against Kutuzov's men, withstanding pressure from the Cossack cavalry and numerous isolated soldiers. The courage of the young guardsmen, led by Roguet, was widely admired, while Davout rushed away from the battlefield.*

*Below:* *The courage and sacrifice displayed during the crossing of the Berezina was overshadowed by the gruelling battle waged by the French and the Poles against Chichagov's troops. The construction of two bridges, under the supervision of General Éblé, allowed most of the soldiers to cross the river. Nevertheless, the loss of 45,000 men stands as one of the most crushing defeats in military history. The name Berezina has passed into the French language as a synonym for "rout".*

water up to their shoulders, the crossing that took place between 26 and 29 November 1812 was soon rendered impossible by the panic that seized the remaining men. The campaign, anticipated as no more than a healthy walk, had become a rout, and the cold added to fear caused the deaths of many hundreds more from the Grande Armée.

The losses caused by the disastrous campaign were enormous throughout Europe, and sowed the seeds of the dissolution of Napoleon's Empire. Those who had perished in Russia were the very German, Italian, and Polish generals, officers and men of the various foreign nations who had put their trust in the emperor and secured for him the loyalty of their compatriots; these were the foreign regiments he had trained for battle, the artillery batteries he had organized, the soldiers who had become accustomed to shouting "Vive l'Empereur!" in every language of Europe and risking their lives for a word of praise from Napoleon in his Bulletins or being rewarded with the Legion of Honour.

Of the 600,000 men who had crossed the Niemen three months earlier, only 60,000 managed to escape. Napoleon later admitted on Saint Helena: "And really, it was due to very few things! But I had gone to fight armed men, not the wrath of nature: I defeated armies, but I could not vanquish the flames, the frost, the numbness and death! Fate was stronger than I."

## Michel Ney (1769–1815)

The man who took part in all the great battles of the Empire leading up to Waterloo is probably most famous for his heroic attitude in Russia. Fighting like a simple grenadier, he was one of the last to cross the Niemen after the terrible Russian campaign. The son of a cooper from Lorraine, his military career had hitherto been exemplary in every respect. He was made a general on the eve of Brumaire, became a marshal on the proclamation of the Empire and distinguished himself at Elchingen, Friedland and Borodino. His many mistakes at Jena and Eylau and his aberrations in Spain should not eclipse the qualities of the man who was nicknamed "the bravest of the brave". Refusing to support the restored monarchy, he instead continued to give allegiance to Napoleon at Waterloo. His subsequent trial for treachery in 1815 – which ended in his execution in the Place de l'Observatoire – was in keeping with his career, revealing those characteristics of loyalty and courage which had kept him steadfast on the field of battle, but got the better of him at the last. His enemies criticized his fits of temper and especially his over-confidence in bringing back Napoleon, who had landed in 1815 "in an iron cage". This action hastened his downfall and some of his former companions (Kellermann, Victor, Sérurier, Perignon and Marmont) condemned him to death.

# The 1813 Campaign

On his return to Paris, Napoleon learned that he had almost lost power following a plot led by General Malet. Although this long-time adversary had been imprisoned at the time of Napoleon's departure, he had succeeded in rallying a few malcontents to his cause and tricked the lower echelons of power into awarding him control of the Paris police. Even the chief ministers were caught in the trap of rumours concerning Napoleon's supposed death in Russia – and no one thought of proclaiming Napoleon's son, the King of Rome, as emperor with the title of Napoleon II.

Imperial power could only be legitimized by victory, and the shock waves resulting from the dramatic events in Russia caused a swing in public opinion. The Grande Armée was no longer invincible. Moreover, the anti-French coalition now included Sweden under Bernadotte, its newly elected crown prince, and Russia, which had continued its offensive in Poland.

The fall of Warsaw to the tsar at the beginning of February, followed by the Russian advance on Berlin, forced the French troops to withdraw, first to the Oder, and then to the Elbe at the beginning of March. The conclusion of an alliance with Frederick William of Prussia added considerable reinforcements to the tsar's armies. After reconstituting his forces, Napoleon left Paris on 15 April. He had barely 200,000 men, including 60,000 Germans who were ready to betray him at the first defeat, and his cavalry, in particular, was far too weak. However, this was leaving the military genius of the "Little Corporal" out of the equation.

Much to everyone's surprise, Napoleon was the victor at Lützen on 2 May, at Bautzen on the 20th, at Würschen on the 21st and Reichenbach on the 23rd. However, the death of Bessières hit the emperor hard, and he had lost many of his troops. With few illusions, he sent Caulaincourt (whose younger brother had been killed at the Battle of Borodino) to Alexander I's headquarters to start negotiations, but the tsar dismissed the emissary, interpreting the French request as a sign of weakness. Austria offered to act as mediator in order to conclude a five-week truce. Under pressure from his entourage, Napoleon made the mistake of accepting. Yet he knew that this was a manoeuvre on Austria's part, prior to betraying him and entering the war on the side of the allies. The Armistice of Pleiswitz was signed on 4 June and was due to expire on 20 July, allowing just enough time for the Russians and Prussians to reorganize, and for the Austrians to make ready to attack. As soon as the agreement was signed, the emperor felt he had made a mistake and apologized, saying, "Berthier and Caulaincourt put pressure on me."

On 9 August, Napoleon received an ultimatum from the Austrian chancellor Metternich, laying claim to three-quarters of the Empire. During the night, he accepted some of the conditions and rejected others, but as Metternich had received nothing by midnight on the 10th, he dissolved the congress. Austria declared war on 11 August. The allied armies now numbered 600,000 men while Napoleon could scarcely assemble 350,000. Many of them were young conscripts, some barely fifteen or sixteen years old. They were called the "Marie-Louise" in honour of the empress, who was regent of the Empire at the time. "We have no cavalry; it does not matter, the French infantry must be able to cope everywhere. I am not afraid to rely on the innate courage of our young conscripts."

Despite their lack of experience, the young troops behaved admirably in battle. Thanks to them, on 27 August the emperor won a brilliant victory at Dresden. By preventing Schwarzenberg, Commander-in-Chief of the Austrian army, from entering Bohemia during a two-day battle, in which he shared the perils and

successes of his young guards, Napoleon dealt his enemies a severe blow; they lost 27,000 men while the French had only 8,000 put out of action. The next day, exhausted and burning with fever, the emperor wrote to Marie-Louise: "I gave Prince Schwarzenberg and Tsar Alexander a good thrashing. The troops of old man Francis [of Austria] have never been so poor …". But Napoleon's joy was short-lived as his marshals were beaten one after the other on the fronts in Silesia and Brandenburg. First Macdonald was defeated at the Katzbach by Blücher, then Oudinot at Grossbeeren. The corps of General Vandamne was annihilated at Kulm. Encircled by the enemy, Napoleon was forced to fight at Leipzig.

**Below:** *The military defeat at Leipzig was devastating. The old allies emerged from the Battle of Nations as avengers of the humiliations at Austerlitz and Friedland; Schwarzenberg had the honour of announcing the great victory to the sovereigns, who rapidly made their way to the battlefield.*

## Karl Philipp von Schwarzenberg (1771–1820)

The generalissimo of the allied armies in 1814 has not achieved the lasting fame of Wellington, Blücher, Nelson or Metternich. However, his career deserves better than the few lines accorded to him by his few biographers. The son of a great Austrian noble family, this intrepid horseman distinguished himself at Neerwinden and then at Hohenlinden during the War of the Second Coalition (1798–1902) against France. Succeeding in maintaining his reputation, despite successive catastrophes at Ulm and Austerlitz, he served for a time as ambassador in St Petersburg, before returning to fight at Wagram, where he was promoted to lieutenant-general. As ambassador to Paris, he was entrusted with the negotiations for the marriage between Napoleon and Marie-Louise. He gave a ball in honour of the bride but many of the guests were killed in a fire, among them his sister-in-law Pauline. In 1812, he led the Austrian armies that served alongside the French during the Russian campaign as far as the Berezina, but the following year he turned his weapons against the French. After the defeat at Dresden, it was he who led the victorious counter-offensive of Leipzig and he was one of the architects of the final victory of the coalition forces.

## Letter from Napoleon to Marie-Louise, October 1813

A few days before the Battle of Leipzig in October 1813, Napoleon informed the Empress Marie-Louise that the army was carrying out manoeuvres, that everything was going well and that if she wrote to him, she should encrypt her letters via Méneval.

**Above:** *His army totally reconstituted, the emperor prepared to return to the fight against the coalition troops. This time, Germany was the place chosen by the allied monarchies to confront the forces of Napoleon; he is shown here in his Leipzig bivouac giving orders from behind his maps.*

The Battle of the Nations, so named because more than ten countries were involved, lasted three days from 16 to 19 October 1813. Barely 180,000 Frenchmen were opposed by more than 320,000 coalition troops, who were constantly receiving reinforcements. The French side lacked both munitions and men. French loss of confidence was aggravated by the treachery, in mid-battle, of the Saxons, Wurtembergers and Hessians. The battle was one of the most terrible scenes of carnage ever witnessed up to that time. The French put up a splendid resistance, but despite their heroism, they did not have enough ammunition and the emperor could not prevent defeat. The French army lost more than 60,000 men, killed or taken prisoner while the allies lost 54,000, dead or injured.

On 19 October, the entire French army retreated and some corps even gave way to panic. The bridges over the Elster were stormed in the most complete disorder. The sappers blew them up too soon and 12,000 Frenchmen were trapped and unable to cross. Most tried to swim across the river, but the current was too strong and many drowned. Poniatowski, appointed marshal the day before, drowned as he tried to cross the Elster on horseback, "buried in his glory, in the downfall of his country". The road to France was now wide open to the enemy armies.

*Opposite: The emperor visits the battlefield alongside Poniatowski, newly promoted Marshal of the Empire. This painting by Suchodolski pays tribute to the unshakeable bonds between France and Poland, symbolized by this friendship between two heroes of the age.*

*Below: Pursued by the enemy at Leipzig, Poniatowski galloped to cross the Elster but drowned in the attempt. He was buried in the mausoleum of the Polish kings in Cracow, alongside those other valiant defenders of the nation, Sobieski and Kosciusko.*

*Below right: Bernadotte, a Marshal of the Empire, later became the Crown Prince of Sweden. Although he once fought beside Napoleon, he later turned his guns against his former comrades-in-arms.*

# Jean Baptiste Jules Bernadotte (1763–1844)

A confirmed republican, General Bernadotte was for a long time an obstacle in Napoleon's path. His marriage to Napoleon's former fiancée Désirée Clary, whose sister had married Joseph Bonaparte, is not the only explanation for their mutual distrust – at any rate it was less important than their differences of opinion and the glory Bernadotte won on the battlefield of Fleurus in the French Revolutionary Wars. Although the opponents of the First Consul and later those opposed to the emperor considered him as someone they could turn to after the departure of Moreau, Bernadotte succeeded in finding favour with Napoleon, becoming one of his first marshals in 1804 and also Duke of Ponte-Corvo. But having been dismissed from decision-making bodies because of his successive mistakes at Jena, Eylau and Wagram, his sudden alliance with the tsar and the British after he had became Prince of Sweden in 1810 assured him a quite different rise to fame. This was confirmed by his coronation when he acceded to the Swedish throne in 1818, under the name of Charles XIV. His descendants still rule in Stockholm today.

# The French Campaign

On 1 January 1814, Napoleon launched a violent attack on the deputies of the Legislature, accusing them of being responsible for more than just military errors : "I had called on you for help and you went and said and did what was necessary to help the foreigners. I am the true representative of the nation. What is the throne? Four pieces of gilded wood covered with velvet? No! The throne is a man, and I am that man!" The next day he sent commissioners into the departments and created the "corps francs". Having re-established the National Guard of Paris, on 23 January he again entrusted the regency to Marie-Louise and presented his son to the officers of the National Guard. All those present were deeply moved and promised to defend the glorious throne of France with their lives. In a voice full of emotion, the emperor told them: "I am leaving you the empress and the King of Rome, my wife and my son. I will leave with my mind free of all anxiety, because they will be in your safe-keeping. All that I hold most dear in the world, after France, I place in your hands." But who could still have believed that the situation could be rescued? Who could have imagined any outcome other than the fall of the regime?

The following day, Napoleon appointed his brother Joseph Lieutenant-General of the Empire. He left the capital during the night of 24 January, after embracing his wife and son for the last time. The coalition had a million armed men, not counting the reserves. Only 60,000 fit men were left in the French ranks. Three enemy armies had already entered France – Bernadotte through Belgium, Blücher across the Vosges and Schwarzenberg via the Plateau de Langres.

Napoleon went straight to Château-Thierry and then to Châlons, where he met up with his marshals. On 26 January, he reached Vitry-le-François, where he took command of his armies. The next day, he won victories at Saint-Dizier and Brienne, where he almost captured Blücher, whom he would meet again eighteen months later at Waterloo.

The emperor was defeated at La Rothière on 1 February, but succeeded in repelling Blücher and Giulay. He went to Troyes and then to Nogent-sur-Seine where, during the night, he received a dispatch from Caulaincourt informing him of the allies' demands. He then went to Sézanne, on the very day when discussions with the allies were broken off. On 10 February, he was the victor at Champaubert and the next day at Montmirail. Catching up with the Russian General Sacken, just as he was endeavouring to join up with the Prussian General Yorck, Napoleon found himself defeated (it is true the odds were against him, facing, as he was, two opponents).

However, Napoleon once more succeeded in working miracles. He defeated Yorck at Château-Thierry, Blücher at Vauchamps, then on 18 February he won a victory at Montereau. During this final day of the initial phase of the campaign, legend would seize on the figure of Napoleon aiming the cannon himself and giving the command to fire. It turned out that several artillerymen were killed at his side. But to those who expressed their anxiety about the risks

The son of a diplomat, Metternich met Napoleon at Rastadt in 1797 and was then posted to Berlin before coming to Paris in 1806. He was an inveterate womanizer, and was reputed to have had numerous liaisons, in particular with Caroline and the future Duchesse d'Abrantès. But the 1809 campaign forced him to leave France in haste. He was present at Wagram and was appointed chancellor after the defeat. After negotiating the marriage of Marie-Louise with the French emperor, he hoped to limit the repercussions of the Treaty of Schönbrunn. However, the failure of his policy forced him to harden his position. In June 1813, he succeeded in convincing the Austrian emperor to rejoin the coalition powers and, after the final victory, organized the Congress of Vienna, which would determine relations between the main European powers for almost thirty years. He remained in power until the revolution of March 1848.

**Opposite:** *This painting by Meissonier adds to the legend of the French campaign. The country was in danger and action had to be taken.*

**Above:** *When the French tried to capture Blücher in Brienne, Napoleon rediscovered places that he had known as a child. Here he was saved by Gourgaud, a young officer who struck down a Cossack intent on attacking the emporer. Gourgaud would follow Napoleon to Saint Helena the following year.*

**Left:** *One of many clocks devoted to the Napoleonic legend, here we see the former gunner taking control of a cannon and directing the manoeuvres himself at Montereau, thereby setting an example for his men.*

incurred, he replied: "Come now, my friend, the bullet that will kill me has not yet been cast."

The following day, he rejected the allies' peace proposals and wrote to his father-in-law, Francis I, to propose different terms "on the basis of Frankfurt". He could not bring himself to accept the unacceptable. "Abandon conquests that were made before my time, leave France smaller than I found her? Never!"

After resuming command of the army and defeating Blücher's vanguard at Méry, he entered Troyes and then joined Mortier and Marmont. He arrived at Jouarre, had the bridge at La Ferté repaired, and then crossed the Aisne at Berry-au-Bac, where he drove off the Cossacks. He repelled Blücher again at Craonne but was himself defeated, this time at Laon, and, on 10 March was forced to retreat to Soissons.

His last great victory was at Reims. The encounters at Épernay, Arcis-sur-Aube and Saint-Dizier only delayed an outcome that most knew to be inevitable. While Napoleon made his way to Fontainebleau, where he was soon forced to abdicate and abandoned by almost all his marshals, Moncey, the only one still fighting the enemy, reached the wall of the fermiers-généraux. Having been appointed Major-General of the National Guard of Paris by the emperor when he left to defend the borders, the former first Inspector-General of the Gendarmerie was the last commander to fight in defence of the capital. Nevertheless, the allies entered Paris when the Senate proclaimed the deposition of the emperor on 2 April, followed the next day by that of the Legislature. This marked the end of the empire that three years previously had numbered 130 départements.

**Below:** *The long processions of soldiers during the 1814 campaign was a chilling sight for the French population. The country had not witnessed fighting on its own soil for over twenty years.*

**Opposite:** *Napoleon and his men confronted the coalition troops in extreme conditions of mud and cold. This painting by Gueldry shows them on 10 February 1814, the night before the Battle of Montmirail, preparing for what would be one of their finest victories during the campaign.*

## Gebhard Leberecht von Blücher (1742–1819)

Without Blücher's sudden (and unexpected) arrival at Waterloo, would the outcome of this battle on 18 June 1815 have been the same? Born in Rostock, the son of a former soldier, Blücher first served in the Swedish armies and even took up arms against the Prussians during the Seven Years War. Having become a zealous servant of his former adversaries, he rose through the ranks to become commander-in-chief of the forces of Frederick William III from 1813. He fought valiantly against the French troops at the battles of Katzbach and Leipzig. After nearly being taken prisoner at Brienne, he entered Paris in 1814 and was then transferred to reserve duties. However, Napoleon's return from Elba caused him to return to the army until the final campaign.

**Above:** *This portrait of the Prussian field marshal Blücher, the famous victor of Waterloo, presents him as a formidable warrior.*

# Betrayal and Abdication

**W**hile the allies occupied Paris, Napoleon addressed the National Guard at Fontainebleau, who replied as one man: "Long live the emperor! To Paris! To Paris!" But on 4 April 1814, the marshals rebelled. Faced with their refusal to continue to fight, Napoleon signed his abdication. He abdicated unconditionally on 6 April and around him the number of defections increased. During the night of 12 April, he attempted to poison himself. He recovered on the 13th and that day signed an agreement, which came to be known as the Treaty of Fontainebleau.

Napoleon confided to Caulaincourt: "No doubt I am suffering, but one of my misfortunes surpasses all others: ending my career by signing a treaty in which I have been unable to stipulate a single general interest, not even a single moral interest such as the preservation of our flags or the continued existence of the Légion d'honneur! Signing a treaty in which I am given money! Ah! Caulaincourt, if it were not for my son, my wife, my sisters, my brothers, Joséphine, Eugène, Hortense, I would tear this treaty into a thousand pieces … To leave France so small, after having received her, how painful!"

On the 19th, the allied commissioners arrived, and on the 20th, the French emperor said farewell to the National Guard. The weather was cold and misty. He went into the courtyard

of the chateau to salute his brave soldiers one last time. The 1st Regiment of grenadiers of the Old Guard, commanded by General Petit, was waiting for him. The soldiers were drawn up in two ranks. Outside, the local populace had gathered in front of the gates.

The deposed emperor was accompanied by his most faithful companions, Cambronne, Drouot and Bertrand. For the last time, he addressed his National Guard: "Soldiers, I am bidding you farewell. For twenty years, I have always met you on the road to honour and glory. You have not ceased to be models of loyalty and bravery …" He stopped, his voice choked, then continued, "Farewell, my children! I would like to press all of you to my heart! Let me at least embrace your general and your flag!"

The emperor walked forward; General Petit, in tears, flung himself into his arms. Then Napoleon kissed the flag, and uttered these final words: "Beloved standard, may this last kiss re-echo in the hearts of all my soldiers. Farewell once more, my old companions, farewell!"

There was great emotion among the oldest men, especially the standard-bearer, who could not hold back his tears. As the Duchesse d'Abrantès reported, "The soldiers appeared less ready to forget their emperor, less keen to abandon the flag of Valmy and Austerlitz. … On the farewell day, these same soldiers were no longer shouting 'long live the emperor' but their tearful eyes, their sombre silence, broken by sobs when Napoleon kissed the vanquished standard, spoke of their love and their pain." Captain Coignet wrote: "All that could be heard was a groan from all the ranks." The emperor walked quickly over to his coach.

On 28 April 1814, Napoleon embarked from Saint-Raphaël for the island of Elba aboard the English frigate the *Undaunted*. He had been given sovereignty over the island plus an annual income of two million francs. His first exile had begun.

On 4 May, the emperor arrived off Porto-Ferrajo, the capital of his new "kingdom", whose landscape was not dissimilar to that of his native Corsica. Taking his seat on board the launch which would take him ashore, he coldly contemplated what he thought would be the "island of rest". When he set foot on land, the civil, military and religious authorities were there, cannons thundered, bells pealed and the local population acclaimed him with cries of "Evviva il imperatore". That same morning, the island's new sovereign issued a benevolent proclamation:

"I have sacrificed my rights in the interests of the fatherland, and I have reserved for myself the sovereignty and possession of the island of Elba, which has been agreed by all the powers. Please inform the inhabitants of the new state of things and that I have chosen their island for my stay in consideration of the mildness of their manners and their climate. Tell them that they will be the constant object of my keenest interests. – Napoleon."

Accompanied by a small escort composed of, among others, General Bertrand, who had been appointed Minister of the Interior and Governor of Civil Affairs, and General Drouot,

Opposite: *Weary and alone after the events leading up to his abdication, a dejected Napoleon is vividly portrayed by the painter Delaroche.*

Below: *Napoleon descends the horseshoe-shaped staircase in Fontainebleau Château – where in his days of glory he had hobnobbed with the great men of Europe – to bid farewell to his soldiers.*

## Auguste Frédéric Louis Viesse de Marmont (1774–1852)

Should Marmont's ultimate betrayal make us forget the long years of loyalty to the emperor? Marmont, who originally came from Châtillon-sur-Seine, met Napoleon at Toulon before becoming a major-general at the age of twenty-four. As one of the principal architects of the Egyptian expedition and the Brumaire coup d'état, he was rewarded with a seat in the Council of State. When war broke out again, he commanded an army corps in 1805, became Governor General of Dalmatia, and was then promoted to the rank of marshal after the Austrian campaign of 1809. After serving as Governor of the Illyrian Provinces, he saw military service again in Portugal, but was defeated at Arapiles. The campaign of 1813 and the French campaign culminated in his defection on 5 April 1814. After being created a Peer of France, he followed Louis XVIII to Ghent and was then appointed Governor of Paris and Ambassador Extraordinary to Russia before dying in Venice.

## Napoleon's second abdication, 1815

Abdicating for the second time, the Emperor passed his power on to his son, Napoleon II, through this Declaration to the French People. The document was signed in the Élysée Palace on 22 June 1815, four days after Waterloo.

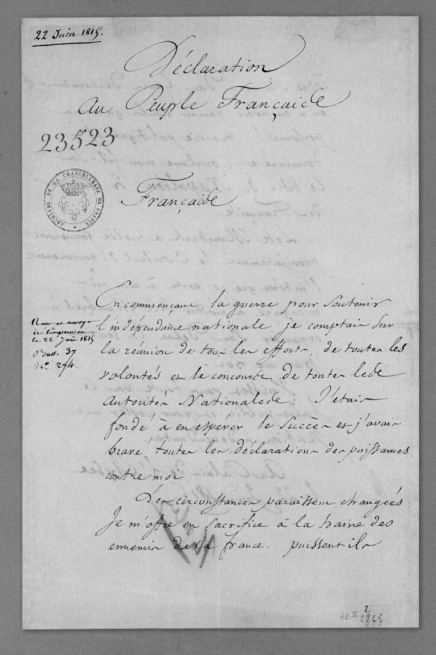

être Sincères dans leur Déclaration
et n'en avoir jamais voulu qu'à ma
personne! ma vie politique est
terminée et je proclame mon fils Sous
le titre de Napoléon 2 Empereur
des Français.

Les Ministres actuels formeront
provisoirement le Conseil de gouvernement.
l'intérêt que je porte à mon fils
m'engage à inviter les Chambres à
organiser Sans délai la régence
par une Loi.

Unissez vous tous pour le
Salut public et pour rester une
Nation indépendante.

Au Palais de l'Élysée
le 22 Juin 1815.

_Napoléon_

## Translation

22 June, 1815.
Declaration to the French people

(in left margin) Received and sent for
printing on June 22, 1815.
Bulletin 37.
No. 274

Frenchmen,
In starting the war to maintain
independence of the nation, I counted
upon uniting all efforts, all wills and the
support of all the national authorities:
I was right to hope for success and I
braved all the declarations of the powers
against me.

The circumstances appear to have
changed: I offer myself as a sacrifice to
the hatred of the enemies of France. Can
they be sincere in their declaration that
they only bore a grudge against me!

My political life is over and I proclaim
my son, under the title Napoleon II,
Emperor of the French.

The present Ministers will form a
provisional council of government.

The interest that I have in my son leads
me to invite this chamber to organize the
regency without delay by means of a law.

All of you, unite for the public safety
and remain an independent nation.

At the Elysée Palace
June 22, 1815

the new Military Governor and Minister of War, Napoleon took up his quarters. Cambronne joined them later, becoming Commander of the Place de Porto-Ferrajo. Napoleon first moved into an apartment prepared for him in the town hall, where he spent a few days. He then took possession of the former governor's palace, the Mulini Palace, where he had a large amount of conversion work done and brought in furniture from the various palaces of his brothers and sisters. This building offered a number of advantages, both for its delightful view over the harbour and the surrounding countryside with its sprinkling of windmills, and its strategic position between the two forts of Porto-Ferrajo.

In addition to this palace, Napoleon looked for a summer residence. His choice fell on a piece of land planted with vines located halfway up mount San Martino, six kilometres from Porto-Ferrajo, and he had a small villa built there.

However, during his first exile, Napoleon was deprived of the company of his wife and his son, the King of Rome. Despite the promises she made in her letters, Empress Marie-Louise never went to the island of Elba, as she was detained in Austria by her father, Francis I.

His sister Pauline visited him on 1 June 1814 and moved into a nearby house five months later. From then on, she helped him to organize parties, balls, receptions and theatrical performances. His former mistress Marie Walewska also paid him a discreet visit, accompanied by their son, and offered him her support and friendship. However, the reunion that aroused the strongest emotions and unprecedented affection in Napoleon was undoubtedly that with Madame Mère, who joined her son on 2 August. Letizia stayed in a house he rented for her in the town, and was the object of every consideration on the part of the sovereign.

Napoleon showed incredible energy in governing his new state. For instance, only two days after his arrival, he went to inspect the iron mines of Rio Marina. With his heart set on the development of his kingdom, he drew up a complete list of the island's resources and launched a plan to build roads linking the towns to the capital, quays and fortifications. He drew up an irrigation plan, advised the growing of potatoes and ordered the replanting of the valleys with olive, mulberry and chestnut trees. He also had the marble quarried, introduced health measures including the building of a hospital and organized the supply of drinking-water to Porto-Ferrajo. He even concluded a trade agreement with Livorno and negotiated another with Genoa.

Right from the start, Napoleon thought about securing his protection. Since the 700 men of his former Guard who wished to follow him into exile did not constitute a sufficiently large force, he decided to "surround himself with a squadron of Polish cavalry, a free battalion of Elba militia and a battalion of Corsican chasseurs", of whom there were many on the island.

This protection was not unnecessary as he remained under the constant surveillance of the men of Louis XVIII (who succeeded him in the Tuileries as King of France) and his allies, including Austria, which had a number of spies deployed on the island. This meant that his every action, even in the privacy of his palace, was scrutinized, deciphered and reported.

For his part, Napoleon kept himself informed about European politics and France. Believing he was in mortal danger and having got wind of a likely royalist plot to assassinate, kidnap, or even deport him, he organized his departure from the island, knowing that he could still count on his close friends and his Guard.

**Above:** *A new flag was chosen for Elba – the white background had a red diagonal stripe set off by three bees.*

**Below:** *On 4 May 1814 the new sovereign was welcomed to Elba by his new subjects in a ceremony distinguished by its warmth and noble simplicity. Who would have guessed four years earlier that the man who reigned over almost all of Europe would have to make do with ruling this small island?*

**Opposite:** *The painter Vernet shows the grenadiers on guard weeping for their emperor as he is embraced by General Petit. Beyond his faithful lieutenants, the foreigners from the commission dispatched by the allies appear to be equally overcome by emotion.*

## Louis-Alexandre Berthier (1753–1815)

Two weeks before Waterloo, Berthier's violent and unexplained death in Bavaria seems an unsatisfactory ending to what had been such a full life. The thinker and chief-of-staff of the Grande Armée and long-serving Minister of War (1799–1807), Berthier had been through the rigorous training of the royal regiments before the revolutionary events that determined his future erupted. Having been associated with major decisions from the time of the first Italian Campaign, he distinguished himself at Lodi and was injured at Marengo before being entrusted with numerous delicate diplomatic missions. Most notably, he was present as a proxy at the marriage of Napoleon and Marie-Louise in Vienna and escorted the new empress to France. His organizational and leadership qualities, rather than his real desire to be involved in the fighting, made him an exemplary assistant. He was rewarded with a great variety of prestigious honours: Master of the Royal Hunt, Grand Eagle of the Legion of Honour, Prince and Vice-Constable.

# The Hundred Days

Evading the surveillance of Colonel Campbell, a Scot charged with reporting Bonaparte's every move to the coalition powers, Napoleon put to sea on the evening of 26 February 1815 on board the brig of the *Inconstant*, arriving at Golfe-Juan on the coast of France on 1 March. The announcement of his arrival hit Vienna and the Tuileries like a bombshell, and triggered a huge popular movement in country areas. The "Little Corporal" was back.

As Napoleon confided to Cambronne, he wanted to "regain the crown without shedding a drop of blood". He passed through Cannes, avoided Grasse and marched straight across the Alps. He entered Digne, Gap and then Laffrey, where he addressed his troops who had come to meet him: "Soldiers of the 5th, I am your emperor, recognize me! If there is a soldier among you who wishes to kill his emperor, he can do so, here I am." Colonel Charles de Labédoyère brought his entire regiment to join them on the Grenoble road.

As Napoleon had planned, his unrelenting progress was made without a single drop of blood being spilt. The proclamation of Golfe-Juan had won people's respect:

"Soldiers, come and form up under the flags of your leader; his existence comprises only your existences; his rights are only yours and those of the people; his interest, his honour, his glory are no different from your interest, your honour and your glory. My victory will proceed at the charge; the eagle, with the national colours, will fly from bell-tower to bell-tower all the way to the tower of Notre-Dame. Then you will be able to show your scars with honour. Then you will be able to take pride in what you have done."

Then he entered Lyon, where he decreed that the tricolore should be restored as the national flag. As he reached Villefranche, Mâcon, Tournus, and then Chalon, his journey became a triumphal progress. During this time Ney, who had been sent by Louis XVIII, changed sides – the "bravest of the brave" would meet up with Napoleon at Pont-sur-Yonne. Napoleon entered Autun, Avallon, and then Auxerre, and on 20 March, carried aloft by his men, he returned to the Tuileries.

In the days that followed, Napoleon put together his new government. He also drew up a list of 13 traitors, including Talleyrand, Marmont, Bourrienne, and Montesquiou, who would no longer have the right to sit at his side or, more importantly, to set foot on French soil again. On 24 March, he abolished censorship. On 4 April, he wrote to the allies to inform them that he accepted the peace treaty. And on 22 April, he issued the Act Additionnal to the Constitutions of the Empire. Even his former opponent Benjamin Constant agreed to offer his services, and the emperor's brother Lucien was reconciled with him, thus regaining all his rights within the imperial family.

After the electoral colleges had been convened in order to elect the Chamber of Representatives, the vast democratic movement became unstoppable. On 1 June, the Assembly of the Champ de Mai met and the results of the plebiscite were announced. Napoleon took the oath. Had it not been for the death of Berthier, the celebration would have been perfect.

Very soon, news arrived from the Belgian border that was not reassuring for the champions of peace. The emperor did not hesitate for a moment. Leaving the Elysée Palace, where he had taken up quarters since his return, he made ready to lead what was to be his last campaign. On 12 June, he assembled his forces to confront the 220,000 coalition troops massing on the borders, in the firm belief that their unity existed only on the surface and that if he attacked each of the enemy armies separately, he would succeed in beating each one in turn. He had only 115,000 men but managed to forestall the enemy without being troubled.

The initial French manoeuvres were a real success. On 15 June they managed to evade the surveillance of the Prussian General Ziethen who was guarding the three crossings over the Sambre at Marchiennes, Charleroi and Le Châtelet. Then, positioned between the headquarters of Wellington and Blücher, Napoleon sent Ney towards the crossroads of Quatre Bras. But the wait-and-see policy and the lack of conviction in its execution almost caused the failure of the cleverly devised plan. At the same time, the Battle of Ligny enabled the French to drive back the Prussians and put some 25,000 enemy soldiers out of action. All that remained was to deal the death blow to the British, who had their backs to the village of Mont-Saint-Jean near Waterloo. It lay at the top of a counterslope that "made it possible to wait for the attack in shelter".

The late start of the battle and, more importantly, the road – later made famous by the poet Victor Hugo – prevented any cavalry charge from reaching its goal. In Murat's absence, Ney led the cuirassiers in an unexpected attack on the English (who had formed compact and orderly squares) at about four in the afternoon. "Come and see how a marshal of France dies", he proclaimed, at the head of his thousands of men whose shouting seemed to drown the deafening noise of the hoof-beats. "The face of this battle was

*Opposite: Led by the sailors of the Guard, Napoleon boarded the Inconstant on 26 February and headed for the French coast, where his partisans eagerly awaited him. Napoleon's arrival at Golfe-Juan would be the first stage of the "flight" of the Eagle "from steeple to steeple, to the towers of Notre Dame".*

*Above: Napoleon arrived in the Tuileries on 20 March 1815, and on 1 June he organized a grand swearing-in ceremony at the foot of the École Militaire, where, a decade earlier, the eagles had been distributed to the armies. This ceremony, known as the "Field of May", was intended to strengthen the bonds between the emperor and his people.*

## Arthur Colley Wellesley, Duke of Wellington (1769–1852)

Though perhaps best known for his part in Napoleon's final defeat at Waterloo, in 1809–13 Wellington led his troops in Portugal and Spain, where he succeeded in repelling the forces of Soult, Masséna and Marmont. He then took the offensive in the south-west of France in 1814. Wellington was associated with the Congress of Vienna, which discussed the fate of Europe after Napoleon's exile on the island of Elba. Consequently, he was once again placed in command of the coalition forces during the Hundred Days. His persistence and his legendary composure enabled him to contain the assault of the French cavalry and hold out at Waterloo until the arrival of Blücher's Prussians. He later turned his prestige as the conqueror of Napoleon to advantage, occupying a number of official positions in Britain, as ambassador, minister and eventually prime minister.

monstrous. These squares were no longer battalions, they were craters; these cuirassiers were no longer a cavalry force, they were a storm. Each square was a volcano attacked by a cloud; lava fought against lightning."

Having countered the successive attacks of the enemy cavalry, Wellington ordered his infantry to break through the lines of the last of Napoleon's forces. At the same time, while Napoleon was waiting for help expected from Grouchy on the right, Blücher and his Prussians finally arrived on the heights of the battlefield after a long battle at Plancenoit. Victory had changed sides.

The Guard had given its all to contain the final British offensives, but the difference in numbers finally demolished the last shreds of hope. The elite of the infantry, the sacred band, had in turn formed squares under the orders of Generals Roguet, Cristiani and Cambronne. According to legend, the latter is said to have replied to an English officer who ordered him to cease fighting, with the famous word for which his name has gone down in posterity, "Shit, the Guard dies but does not surrender." The return of the combatants, however, meant that there was no prospect of any solution other than an orderly withdrawal.

Forced to give up, Napoleon signed his second abdication, this time at the Elysée Palace, on 22 June 1815:

"Declaration to the people of France: Frenchmen, when I began the war to maintain national independence, I was counting on uniting all efforts, all wills, and on the support of all the national authorities. I had reason to hope for its success, and I had defied all the declarations of the powers against me. Circumstances appear to have changed. I offer myself as a sacrifice to the hatred of the enemies of France. May they be sincere in their declarations and their resentment only ever have been against me personally! My political life is over, and I proclaim my son Emperor of France, with the title of Napoleon II.

The current ministers will provisionally form the ruling council. The interest I have in my son's welfare urges me to ask the chambers without delay to establish the regency by law. Unite, all of you, for the public safety and in order to remain an independent nation. Napoleon."

After leaving Malmaison and bidding farewell to his stepdaughter Hortense, he passed through Rochefort and Fouras, landing on the Island of Aix on 8 July 1815. It was to be his last stay on French soil.

*Left: While Napoleon was waiting for Grouchy's arrival on his right wing, it was Blücher's Prussians who were really advancing on the battlefield. Despite the French heroism and the sacrifice of the Guard, defeat was unavoidable.*

*Below: Lucien's second marriage had led to a rift with his brother Napoleon that lasted for over ten years but they were reconciled for the Hundred Days. Their long conversations in the Élysée forged this new adventure, reminiscent of the great days of the Consulate.*

## Emmanuel de Grouchy (1766–1847)

The last marshal of the Empire, appointed on the eve of Waterloo, deserves better than the caricature that has been handed down by legend and the dreadful verdict accorded him by Napoleon in the *Mémorial*: "Marshal Grouchy, with 34,000 men and 108 cannons, discovered the apparently undiscoverable secret of not being on the battlefield either at Mont-Saint-Jean or at Wavre during the day on the 18th ... Marshal Grouchy's conduct was as unpredictable as if his army had been engulfed by an earthquake along the way." His fatal absence during the final confrontation should not cause us to forget the success of his career, which began under the ancien régime and was later acknowledged at Ulm, Lübeck, Eylau, Friedland and then at Raab and Wagram. His role in the Russian campaign was among the most important, especially at Borodino, Malo-Jaroslavets and when he saved the elite squadron during the dramatic retreat. He then distinguished himself at Brienne and Montmirail, having been dismissed in 1813 for refusing the appointment imposed on him by the emperor. His "absence" at the end should not cause us to forget his vital role during the Hundred Days and at the Battle of Ligny.

# Saint Helena

Probably expecting to be exiled to the United States with his brother Joseph, Napoleon surrendered to the English. He wrote to the Prince Regent, "Having become the target of the factions dividing my country and the hostility of the greatest powers in Europe, I have ended my political career. I have come like Themistocles to make my home among the British people; I place myself under the protection of its laws, which I request of Your Royal Highness as the most powerful, constant, and noble of my enemies."

Though he may have believed he would be allowed to live in England, he was finally exiled to Saint Helena, an isolated island in the middle of the Atlantic, 3,500 kilometres (2,174 miles) from Brazil and 2,500 kilometres (1,553 miles) from the coast

**Below:** *On board the* Northumberland, *Napoleon set sail for Saint Helena accompanied by the last of his followers. He saluted the coast of France one last time.*

**Right:** *Exiled once again, this time to the middle of the South Atlantic, Napoleon was introduced to the place that he had described as a child in a notebook as "Saint Helena, small island".*

## Henri Gatien, Comte Bertrand (1773–1844)

Bertrand, the emperor's last companion on Saint Helena in his capacity as Grand Marshal of the Palace, was one of the most brilliant officers of the Grande Armée. A former officer of the Garde Nationale de Paris, he had a ringside seat at the storming of the Tuileries on 10 August 1792. After fighting in the war of the Pyrenees, he participated in the first Italian campaign and the Egyptian expedition, where he distinguished himself at Aboukir Bay. He then appeared at Austerlitz, Jena, Eylau and Wagram before becoming Governor General of the Illyrian Provinces. Appointed in 1813 to succeed Duroc, he shared both of Napoleon's island exiles. In 1840, he commanded the *Belle Poule* on the expedition to return the emperor's ashes, before dying in his native town of Châteauroux.

of Africa. There he lived out his last years with a few companions who had agreed to share his exile. The French emperor would exhaust the last of his strength in this windy and rainy hell, under the close supervision of the English governor, Hudson Lowe.

When Napoleon arrived on the island of Saint Helena on 17 October 1815, he was accompanied by a few loyal men, some of whom he really didn't know very well. Unlike Grand Marshal Bertrand, he had rarely encountered Generals Montholon and Gourgaud. Bertrand and Montholon were accompanied by their wives, Albine (who is said to have had a liaison with Napoleon) and Fanny. A dozen servants also sailed to Saint Helena, among them Louis Marchand, Napoleon's chief manservant, and Emmanuel Las Cases, his chamberlain.

When he first arrived on the island, Napoleon was lodged in a summer residence on the Briars estate belonging to William Balcombe, a merchant of the East India Company. In the space of two months, he formed an attachment to his host's daughter Betsy, whose friendship made the initial period of his exile more bearable. But on 10 December he was moved to Longwood House, a secluded building at one end of the island, and it was here that his true imprisonment commenced. The house was spartan, damp and confined. It consisted of a parlour, a drawing-room, a dining-room, two bedrooms and a study. His retinue had to make do with hastily constructed buildings made of mud and stone. This was where Napoleon's descent into hell began.

Governed by strict regulations and under constant supervision, life stretched out monotonously for all the occupants who were overcome by gloom, pettiness and jealousy Napoleon now lived the life of a recluse. The man who was once able to sleep on a simple drum suffered agonies of insomnia. He would shut himself away for weeks on end and rarely went out. The days dragged on, each the same as the previous one. He only allowed himself an occasional ride, accompanied by Gourgaud or Las Cases.

Napoleon insisted that his companions should always be available, but at the same time he suffered from their incessant quarrelling. Dinner, which they ate together, gave the illusion of civility when they got out the Sèvres porcelain, the silverware and the gold place-settings. However, relations between the captives deteriorated rapidly and Bonaparte's health gradually declined. The unpredictability of the climate, the constant humidity and the poor sanitary conditions caused strange symptoms – violent migraines, constipation, swollen ankles, photophobia (so bad that Napoleon insisted the shutters should always be closed), gingivitis, alternating bouts of somnolence and insomnia, an uncontrollable cough … At the end of 1816, Marchand noted in his memoirs: "The emperor's health has seriously deteriorated."

**Opposite below left:** *Napoleon had many long hours to ponder his extraordinary career: "What a destiny my life has been!"*

**Below:** *In the clammy atmosphere of Longwood, Napoleon dictated to Las Cases what would soon become the hugely successful Memorial of Saint Helena. This exceptional publishing event would inspire a whole generation of Romantic writers, from Hugo to Balzac, and from Lamartine to Sir Walter Scott.*

## Sir Hudson Lowe (1769–1844)

On 14 April 1816, Lowe arrived on Saint Helena. As the new governor, he was charged with ensuring that Napoleon's sentence was carried out. An Irish-born officer from a relatively humble background and eaten up with ambition, Lowe was intelligent but terribly cold. He quickly made himself hated by both the French and his compatriots. Even Wellington said of him, "He is not a gentleman". He fulfilled his mission zealously and without weakening. For Lowe, guarding Napoleon was a magnificently glorious mission. As soon as he arrived, he put in place numerous regulations, restrictions and bans. In five years, the jailer and his prisoner saw each other only five times; these meetings turned into verbal joustings which only made the conditions of the emperor's captivity harder. After Napoleon's death, Hudson Lowe left the island with a feeling of duty done, but fate caught up with him and he ended his life in great misery.

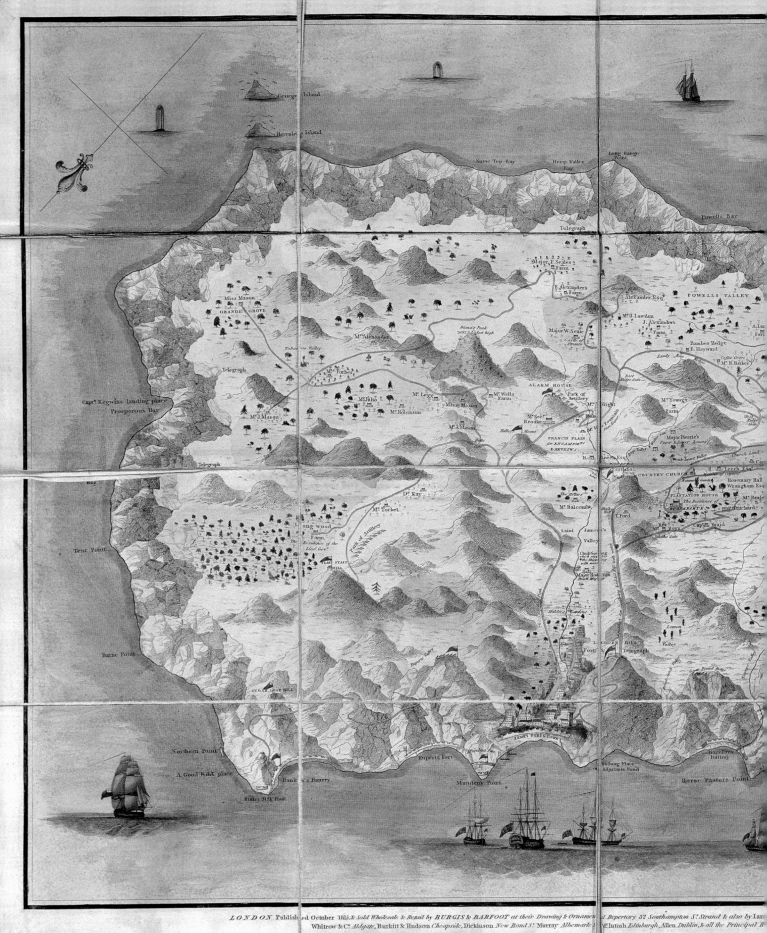

George's Island

Hercules's Island

Stone Top Bay    Deep Valley Bay    Long Range Point

Powells Bay

Telegraph

Major E Seales Farm

F. Alexander's Farm    Green Hill    Alexander Esq    POWELLS VALLEY

Miss Mason    Mr J. Lowden    A La

ORANGE GROVE    J. Alexander Farm    Fa

Mrs Alexander    Major W. Seale    Castle of Otranto    Bamboo Hedge    E. Hayward

Blunt's Peak    2697 Feet high    Mr R Baker

Tobacco Valley    Sandy Bay    Mr Youngs Farm

Telegraph    Mr Forbes    Mr Legg    Mr Wells Farm    ALARM HOUSE    Park of Artillery    Wright    Well

Capt. Kegwins landing place    Mr John    Miss Mason    Mr See Brooke    Buh    Mount    Major Pierrie's

Prosperous Bay    Mr J Mason    Mr Robinson    FRANCIS PLAIN    for ENCAMPMT & REVEIWS    Upper & Lower Romey

Mr J Mason    Halley    CITADEL    COUNTRY CHURCH

Telegraph    Leech Esq    Rosemary Hall    Wrangham Esq

Dr Kay    PLANTATION HOUSE    Mr Beale

Mr Torbet    The BF'st    BONAPARTE    Mr Pritchard

Tent Point    Long wood Farm    Mr Balcomb    The Residence of    Rev    Capt Braid

The Residence of the    T. Ford    Saint    James's    Valley

Lieut Govr    Park of Artillery    Cold Spring

FLAG STAFF HILL    Major Hodson    Lemon

Barne Point    Gardens    Valley

SUGAR LOAF HILL    LADDER HILL    Fort    Telegraph

Ruperts Valley    JAMES FORT & TOWN

Northern Point    Ruperts Fort    Bathing Place    Banks Battery

A Good Fish g place    Mundens Point    Adjutants Pond    Horse Pasture Point

Banks's Battery    Butter Milk Point

LONDON Published October 1815 & Sold Wholesale & Retail by BURGIS & BARFOOT at their Drawing & Ornamental Repertory 32 Southampton St Strand & also by Lux
Whitrow & Co Aldgate, Burkitt & Hudson Cheapside, Dickinson New Bond St. Murray Albemarle St McIntosh Edinburgh, Allen Dublin, & all the Principal B

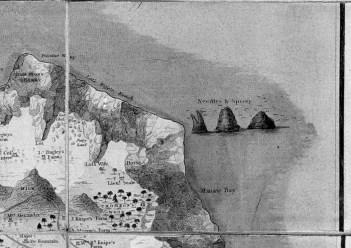

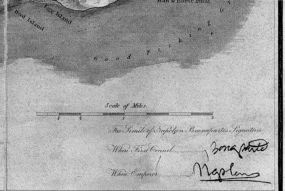

## Map of Saint Helena

Despite the geographical difficulties of the time, this letter from
Saint Helena signed by the Emperor's own hand indicates the main
places on the island, including Longwood, Jamestown and the Briars.

# Death

From 1817, Napoleon suffered from dysentery and rheumatic pains. He had more and more difficulty walking. During a slight improvement in 1819 he tried to take an interest in gardening, but sank back into extreme melancholia. His ill-health returned in the middle of 1820 and Doctor Antommarchi was unable to help him. Grand Marshal Bertrand noted: "This illness has nothing in common with his previous liver trouble." The illness got worse. He had frequent attacks of vomiting, the stomach pains became more acute and he could hardly walk. Hudson Lowe turned a deaf ear. For him it was "a disease of the mind and not of the body; the result of his bad behaviour towards me". The progress of the illness was frightening – abdominal pain on the right side, fever, coughing, icy cold in the legs. At the beginning of 1821, the Emperor took to his bed and never left it again.

On 21 April Napoleon began to make detailed plans for the organization of the religious ceremonies surrounding his death, which he knew was close. He ordered that a "chambre ardente" should be set up close to his bed. On 3 May he became delirious. On the 4th, violent tropical rains beat down on the island, but abated the next day, 5 May, which was to see the end of everything.

On that day, Antommarchi prescribed calomel, an emetic containing antimony, which further weakened the emperor. He then ordered a drink flavoured with bitter almonds, which proved equally harmful to the dying patient.

"My son … head of the army": the last words spoken by Napoleon before he died on 5 May 1821 at 5.49 p.m. were those of a man abandoned by his relatives and friends who had lost

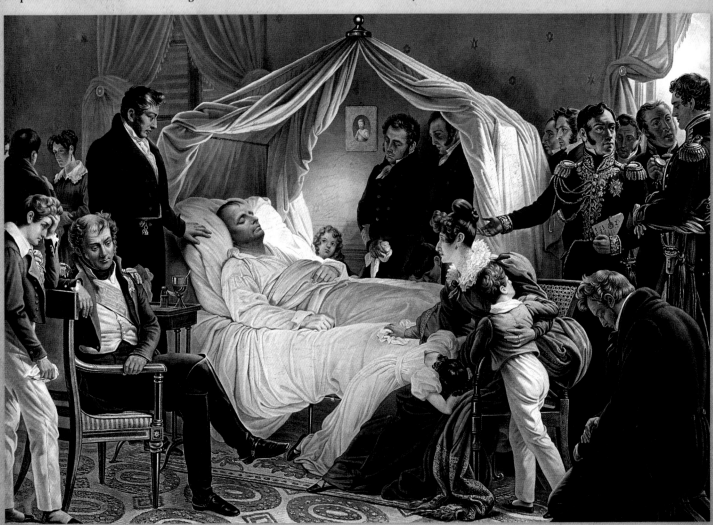

Was Montholon so jealous of his wife Albine's liaison with Napoleon that he wished to poison him? Whatever the truth, this is how posterity presents him. After serving in the navy and distinguishing himself during the 18 Brumaire uprising, he participated in a number of Napoleon's campaigns and was wounded at Essling. As brigadier-general he took command of the département of Loire. He was adjutant general during the Hundred Days, fought bravely at Waterloo, and did not hesitate to accompany the emperor to Saint Helena, taking his wife and children with him. It seems that Napoleon found consolation with Albine, and the physical resemblance of her youngest daughter, Joséphine, to the deposed emperor was probably not coincidental.

Montholon's career did not come to an end in 1821. He reappeared fifteen years later during the attempted coup d'état of Louis-Napoleon (later Napoleon III) at Boulogne-sur-Mer, as a result of which he was imprisoned in the castle of Ham. Having become a deputy in 1849, he died early on in the Second Empire.

absolutely everything. At the age of just 51, his life ended in emotional destitution. According to the terms of his will, he asked for his ashes to be laid to rest in France, to be precise "on the banks of the Seine, in the midst of the French people, whom I loved so much".

His final companions, who had followed him into exile in the middle of the South Atlantic – Bertrand, his wife Fanny and their children; the Comte de Montholon; the manservant Marchand; Doctor Antommarchi; and the Mameluke Ali – bowed their heads at Napoleon's deathbed and paid their final homage.

The emperor was buried in his uniform of the Imperial Guard, not far from Longwood at the bottom of the "Geranium Valley" where he had loved to meditate. The simple tombstone had no inscription – in a final insult, Hudson Lowe did not allow an epitaph to be engraved upon it.

**Opposite:** *After Napoleon's death, his final companions kept watch over the man who, according to Chateaubriand, had just rendered up "the most powerful breath of life that had ever animated human clay". This painting by Steuben recalls the emotional scene on 5 May 1821 when British officers were shown Napoleon's corpse by Montholon.*

**Above:** *After his captive's death, Hudson Lowe allowed the body to be buried in Geranium Valley, a lush area where Napoleon used to enjoy taking long walks. The site is now a major attraction for visitors to the island.*

# Codecil to Napoleon's will

Will and Testament signed by Napoleon, requesting that his ashes be laid to rest by the River Seine. This wish was ignored and he was buried on the island.

**Translation**

This is a codicil to my will and testament all written by my own hand.

[signature] Napoleon

April 16, 1821  Longwood Fifteenth page

[signature]

This is a codicil to my will and testament.
1. I desire that my ashes rest beside the Seine among the French people whom I loved so much

2. I bequeath to Counts Bertrand, Montholon and Marchand the money, jewels, silver, china, furniture, books, weapons, etc. and in general everything that belongs to me on the island of Saint Helena.
This codicil entirely written by my hand is signed and sealed with my crest.

[signature] Napoleon

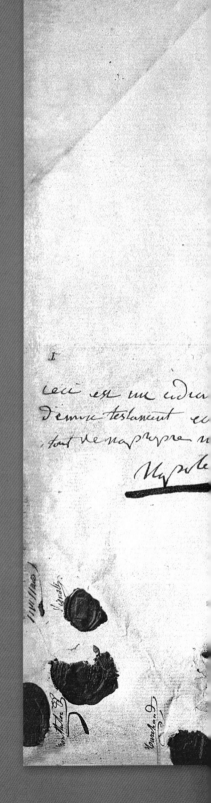

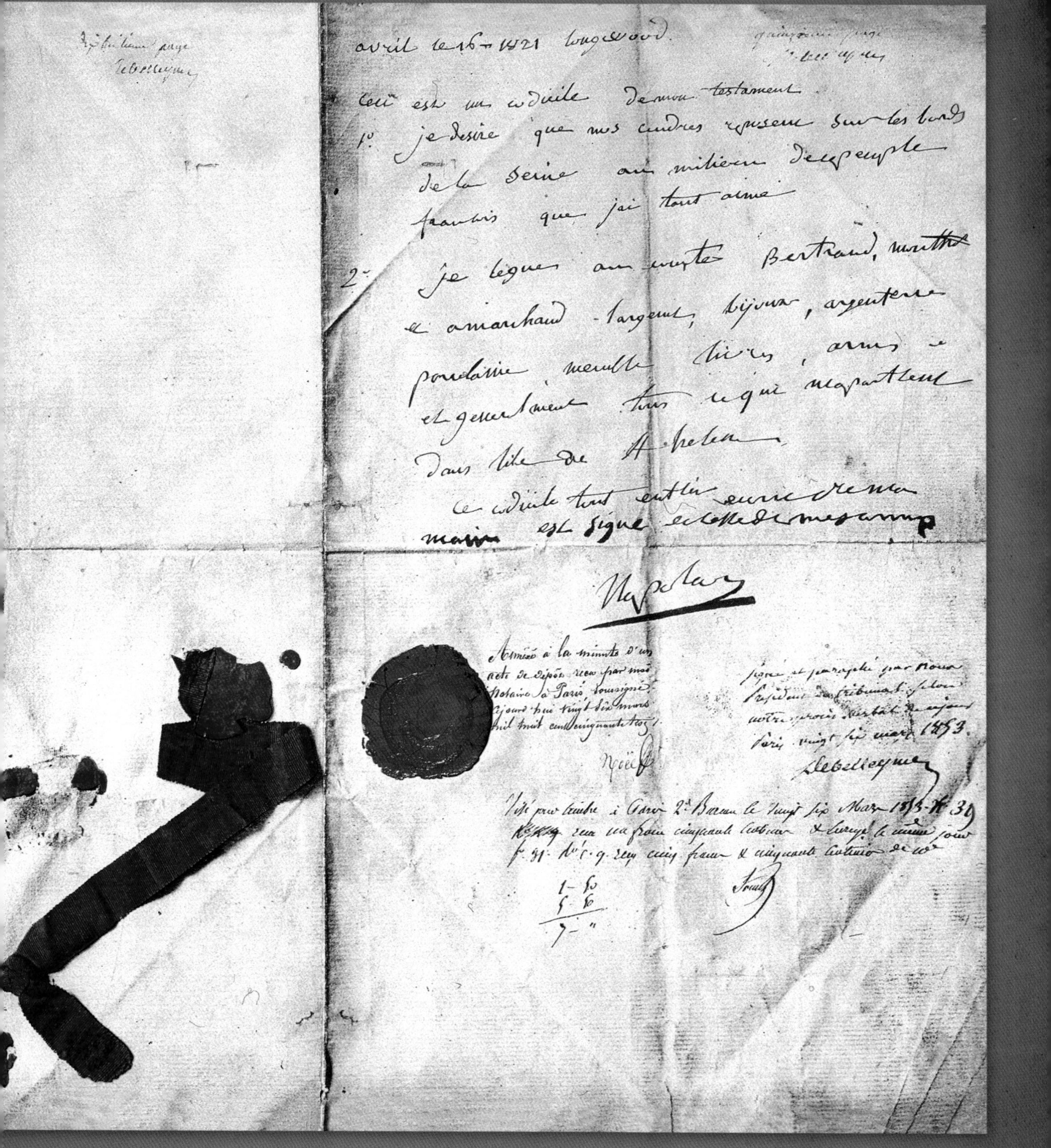

avril le 16 — 1821 Longwood.

Ceci est un codicile de mon testament.

1° je désire que mes cendres reposent sur les bords
de la Seine au milieu de ce peuple
français que j'ai tant aimé

2° je legue au comte Bertrand, mon lit
et marchand, l'argent, bijoux, argenterie,
porcelaine, meuble, livres, armes, et
généralement tous ce qui m'appartient
dans l'île de Ste Hélène

Ce codicile tout entier écrit de ma
main est signé et cacheté de mes armes

*Napoléon*

Annexé à la minute d'un
acte de dépôt reçu par moi
notaire à Paris, soussigné
aujourd'hui vingt six mars
mil huit cent cinquante trois

signé et paraphé par Nous
Président du tribunal, selon
notre procès verbal de ce jour
Paris vingt sept mars 1853
Lebesseyne

Visé pour timbre à Paris 2e Bureau le vingt six Mars 1853 № 30

# Napoleon's postmortem results, 1821

Autopsy report, written by the British surgeons present on Saint Helena, 6 May 1821

**Translation**

At Helena
Longwood 6th May 1821

Report of appearances on dissection of the body of Napoleon Bonaparte.

On a superficial view the body appeared very fat which state was confirmed by the first incision down its centre, where the fat was upwards of one inch thick over the stomach and one inch half over the abdomen. On cutting through the cartilages of the ribs and exposing the cavity of the thorax, a trifling adhesion of the left pleura had bound to the pleura costalis. About three ounces of reddish fluid were contained in the left cavity and nearly eight ounces in the right. The lungs were quite sound. The pericardium was natural and contained about an ounce of fluid.

The heart was of the natural size but thickly covered with fat. The auricles and ventricles exhibited nothing extraordinary except that the muscular parts appeared rather paler than natural.

Upon opening the abdomen, the omentum was found remarkably fat, and on exposing the stomach that viscera was found the seat of extensive diseases; strong adhesions connected the superior surfaces, particularly about the pylorus extremity to the concave surface of the left lobe of the liver, and on separating these, an ulcer which penetrated the coats of the stomach was discovered one inch from the pylorus, sufficient to allow the passage of the little finger. The internal surface of the stomach to nearly its whole extent was a mass of cancerous diseases or schirrous portions advancing to cancer, this was particularly noticed near the pylorus – The cardiac extremity for a small space near the terminations of the oesophagus was the only part appearing in a healthy state. The stomach was found nearly filled with such a large quantity of fluid resembling coffee grounds.

The convex surface of the left lobe of the liver adhered to the diaphragm – with the exception of the adhesions occasioned by the disease in the stomach no unhealthy appearance presented itself in the liver.

The remainder of the abdominal viscera were in a healthy state. A slight peculiarity in the formation of the left kidney was observed.

Thomas Shortt MD
Phys(ician) & P(rincipal) M(edical) O(fficer)
Arbuthnott MD
Surgeon 20th Regiment
Charles Mitchell MD
Surgeon of HMS Vigo
Francis Burton MD
Surgeon 60th Regiment
[Illegible] Livingstone
Surgeon
M. [?] Service

that viscera was found the seat of extensive disease; strong adhesions connected the whole superior surface particularly about the Pyloric extremity, to the concave surface of the left lobe of the liver, and on separating them, an ulcer which penetrated the coats of the Stomach was discovered one inch from the Pylorus sufficient to allow the passage of the little finger. The internal surface of the Stomach to nearly its whole extent was a mass of cancerous disease or schirrous portions advancing to cancer, this was particularly noticed near the pylorus. — The Cardiac extremity for a small space near the termination of the œsophagus was the only part appearing in a healthy state. The Stomach was found nearly filled with a large quantity of fluid resembling Coffee grounds.

The Convex surface of the left lobe of the liver adhered to the diaphragm. — With the exception of the adhesion occasioned by the disease in the Stomach no unhealthy appearance presented itself in the liver. —

The remainder of the abdominal viscera were in a healthy state. —

A slight peculiarity in the formation of the left kidney was observed. —

Thomas Thorn M.D.
Surg. S.P. M.D.

Robert Armstrong M.D.
Surgeon 20th Regt.

Charles Mitchell M.D.
Surgeon of HMS Sloop

Francis Burton M.D.
Surgeon 66th Regt.

Matthew Livingstone
Surgeon
HM of Prisons

In this apotheosis of Napoleon, the painter Horace
Vernet portrays the prisoner as a martyr, mourned
on his rock just as Christ was on Golgotha.

## Francesco Antommarchi (1789–1838)

Antommarchi, a Corsican doctor and anatomist, is chiefly remembered for his dubious choice of remedies administered to Napoleon on Saint Helena. He took on treatment of the prisoner after O'Meara, and cared for him conscientiously for a short time. During the final months, his medical prescriptions did not have the desired effect and his final act was to administer a fatal dose of calomel. During the autopsy, he made copious notes, in which historians and specialists have discovered many inconsistencies. His death in Cuba was preceded by the appearance of his memoirs in 1825. Despite some exaggeration, these constitute an important source of information on the last months of Napoleon's life.

# Napoleon's Legacy

**T**he popular success of La Cases's *Mémorial de Sainte-Hélène*, published in 1823, helped to spread the legend of Napoleon – a legend that first took root in people's minds in the early days of the epic Siege of Toulon and the first Italian campaign.

All of Europe was influenced by a vast literary and artistic movement that spread in a variety of ways – from the greatest works of Hugo, Balzac and Tolstoy to popular prints and the decoration of cheap snuff-boxes.

It was Adolphe Thiers, President of the Council, who proposed that Napoleon's ashes be repatriated to France – this had long been the desire of Napoleon's final companions on Saint Helena. In October 1840 a number of them accompanied the Prince de Joinville, the son of Louis-Philippe, to Elba aboard the *Belle Poule* to retrieve Napoleon's coffin. After a long voyage, the coffin was transferred to a second boat that sailed up the Seine as far as Courbevoie. On 15 December the catafalque was conveyed in a hearse to its final resting place at Les Invalides.

The words spoken by Marshal Moncey – the former Inspector-General of the Gendarmerie under the Empire and later Governor of the Invalides – to his doctor will be remembered as a last symbolic act. Before the ceremony, the patient had begged, "Let me live a little longer. I want to receive the emperor." And in the evening, when the body had been taken down into the crypt of the church, his duty done, he said to his physician, "Now, let us return home to die."

From Rémusat's speech calling for the repatriation of Napoleon's remains to Richard Wagner's underrated recollections of the day itself, the triumphant arrival inspired many writings, each more moving than the last. But if we were to keep only one of them, it would probably be these last lines of Victor Hugo: "Oh! brille dans l'histoire, / Du funèbre triomphe impérial flambeau / Que le peuple a jamais te garde en sa mémoire, / Jour beau comme la gloire, / Froid comme le tombeau! (Oh, shine in history, imperial torch of the funereal triumph, may the people always keep you in their memory, day as bright as glory, cold as the grave.)

**Above:** *An expedition led by the Prince of Joinville was sent to Saint Helena to exhume Napoleon's body. On 15 October 1840, Bonaparte's final companions were surprised to find that his corpse, laid to rest nineteen years earlier, was very well preserved.*

**Opposite:** *On 15 December 1840, Napoleon's coffin arrived in France amidst great popular fervour. The imperial bier's route along the Seine up to its entrance into the dome of the Invalides was lined with adoring crowds, as described by Victor Hugo in* Choses vues.

The lithographs of Raffet, the songs of Béranger and Débraux and the poems of Barthélemy and Méry spread the image of the emperor dressed in his greatcoat, wearing his cocked hat, leather boots and gloves, his hand tucked in his waistcoat, his gaze proud or disillusioned depending on events. His sword always appears at his left side, a sign of his power. There were to be no more depictions of him in his coronation robes – too monarchist, not sufficiently "of the people". The poet Alfred de Vigny was one of the first to define the symbolic significance of this image. "I belong to the generation born at the start of the century who, fed on bulletins by the emperor, always saw before us a drawn sword and seized it at the very moment when France was about to replace it in the scabbard of the Bourbons." And Barbey d'Aurevilly confirms its importance for the fetishist generation of the Romantics: "He had spent his youth getting through an enormous quantity of white gloves and reflecting on life, the only two resources remaining to us young people who have not seen Napoleon."

Thanks to retrospective exhibitions organized around the world, the figure of the emperor has never been more present. Inspiring great politicians and fascinating the most diverse nations, he has probably never been more discussed than he is today.

Cinema and television have made good use of the easily recognizable image of Bonaparte, a "branding" of Napoleon's image that allows us to free the images from any real connection with historical events. The paintings and representations provide an interesting source for film directors as they try to imagine and recreate the Siege of Toulon, the bridge at Arcole, the Battle of the Nile, the crossing of the Saint-Bernard Pass, the

Born in the Tarn region, Marie-Joseph-Emmanuel-Auguste-Dieudonné, Comte de Las Cases, like Napoleon was educated at the École Militaire in Paris. However, unlike Bonaparte, he chose to join the navy. On Martinique, his meeting with Joséphine was one of the great moments of his life. Despite the years spent abroad at the start of the Revolution, especially in London, he took advantage of the amnesty to return to France, where he was made first Baron, then Count of the Empire. He was appointed chamberlain to the emperor in 1809, then Master of Requests in the Council of State. He chose to follow Napoleon to Saint Helena, where his knowledge of English proved invaluable. During the crossing he began writing a journal which he continued until the end of his stay in November 1816. Together with his son who had accompanied him, he then signed what was to become one of the most important documents of the Napoleonic legend, the *Mémorial de Sainte-Hélène*. As deputy for Saint-Denis, he was present at the repatriation of Napoleon's ashes in 1840, dying two years later in Passy.

coronation and the farewells at Fontainebleau. In the eternal figure of the conqueror and sovereign, this process of "narrative representation" becomes effective too, enabling a scene to immediately be put into context. From Albert Dieudonné to Marlon Brando, and from Rod Steiger to Philippe Torreton, actors have perpetuated the memory of the man whose destiny Chateaubriand summed up better than anyone: "In life, he lost the world, in death, he possessed it".

**Opposite:** *The figure of Napoleon was often used to preside over the revolutionary events of 1848. The Saint Helena Memorial presented the emperor as the standard bearer of liberty.*

**Above:** *Few political leaders and heads of state have denied their admiration for Napoleon. Winston Churchill's office is a perfect illustration of this.*

**Below:** *The black felt bicorne hat, an essential component of Napoleon's image, has become an unmistakable trademark in its own right.*

## Napoleon François Charles Joseph Bonaparte, "l'Aiglon" (1811–1832)

Born under the gilded ceilings of the Tuileries Palace in 1811, the man whom Rostand immortalized in his play *l'Aiglon* (*The Eaglet*) had a very tragic life. Although he was brought up with all the honour due to his rank, at the age of three he was taken from his father. After his father abdicated in his favour on 22 June 1815, he was on the throne for only a few hours under the name of Napoleon II. The young boy was then forced to accompany his mother Marie-Louise to Austria, to the castle of Schönbrunn, where his grandfather determined he should have a military career. His sudden death at the age of twenty-one prevented him from having any part in a possible Napoleonic restoration and made him a martyr in the eyes of those loyal to the regime. The return of his ashes to Les Invalides on 15 December 1940, 100 years to the day after his father's but during the dark days of the Nazi occupation, was one of the final humiliations of his tragic destiny.

# Index

# Credits

The publishers would like to thank the following sources for their kind permission to reproduce the photographs in this book.

Key: t = top, b = bottom, l = left, r = right and c = centre

**AKG-Images:** 17 (r), 39; /Electa: 64-65

**Bibliothéque nationale de France:** 112-113, 144-145

**Bridgeman Images:** 7 (r), 13 (t), 15 (b), 16, 18 (t), 19 (r), 34 (t), 36-37, 37 (t), 41 (r), 44-45, 47 (t), 47 (b), 48-49, 53, 54, 56, 57, 61 (r), 62, 62-63, 63, 65 (t), 67 (r), 68, 68-69, 69, 74-75, 75 (r), 76 (r), 76 (b), 81 (t), 81 (r), 88-89, 92 (t), 93 (b), 94-95, 96, 97 (r), 98, 101 (b), 104, 105 (t), 105 (b), 106 (t), 106 (b), 107, 108-109, 109, 114, 115 (l), 115 (r), 116, 117 (r), 118 (t), 124, 125 (r), 126, 127 (t), 127 (b), 130, 131 (r), 134, 135 (r), 136 (l), 137 (r), 138-139, 139 (r), 140-141, 142-143, 146, 152-153, 155 (r), 156, 157 (t)

**Getty Images:** Blue Lantern Studio: 28; /The Gallery Collection: 23 (t); /Hulton-Deutsch Collection: 39 (l)

**National Archives of the U.K. (P.R.O.), Kew:** 150-151

**National Archives of France:** 42, 70, 90-91, 110-111, 132-133

**Photo12.com:** Pierre-Jean Chalencon: 20-21, 30, 102, 122; /ARJ: 50, 77

**Réunion des Musées Nationaux:** 7 (l), 10, 12, 16-17, 19 (t), 25 (br), 27 (br), 28 (t), 41 (t), 60-61, 61 (c), 66, 98-99, 117 (t), 118 (l), 123, 129 (t), 131 (l), 139 (b), 140 (l), 142 (l), 146 (l), 154, 155 (t), 157 (bc), 157 (br); /Gerard Blot: 109 (bc), 118 (r), 127 (b), 128-129 (b), 136; /Agence Bulloz: 99 (r), 148-149; /Daniel Arnaudet/Hervé Lewandowski: 46; /Michéle Bellot: 58-59; /Jean-Gilles Berizzi: 75 (t); /Domaine de Chantilly: 89 (br); /André Martin: 67 (l); /MDA: 80-81, 120-121, 125 (l), 134 (t), 134 (b); /Droits réservés: 55 (br), 92, 100, 118 (b); /Jean Schormans: 8-9; /Château de Versailles: 37 (r), 39 (r), 49 (br), 84-85, 88 (t), 89 (t), 97 (t), 101 (t)

**REX/Shutterstock:** The Art Archive: 26-27 (b), 34 (b), 40-41 (bc), 45 (br), 47 (r), 49 (t), 55 (t)

**Service historique de la Defénse, department de l'armée de terre, Paris:** 82-83, 86-87

**Superstock:** 9 (r)

**Topfoto.co.uk:** 24-25 (b); /The Granger Collection: 18-19, 22 (bl), 22-23, 25 (t) 32-33, 55 (bc), 143 (r); /HIP: 52-53; /Roger Viollet: 6, 9 (b), 13 (b), 14, 24 (t), 27 (t), 28 (b), 32, 35 (l), 35 (r), 78, 121 (r) 141 (r), 147 (br), 153 (r); /Ullstein Bild: 15 (t), 129 (br)

Every effort has been made to acknowledge correctly and contact the source and/or copyright holder of each picture and Carlton Books Limited apologizes for any unintentional errors or omissions, which will be corrected in future editions of this book.